PROTECTING OUR RIGHTS

PROTECTING OUR RIGHTS

BILL VINCENT

CONTENTS

1 Legal Disclaimer   1

2 Introduction   3

3 Chapter 1: Understanding the First Amendment   21

4 Chapter 2: Public Buildings and Spaces   41

5 Chapter 3: The Fourth Amendment and Privacy Concer 63

6 Chapter 4: Recording Private Businesses from Publi   79

7 Chapter 5: Practical Tips for First Amendment Audi   101

8 Chapter 6: Positive Impacts of First Amendment Aud 123

9 Conclusion   141

Copyright © 2024 by Bill Vincent
All rights reserved. No part of this book may be reproduced in any manner whatsoever without written permission except in the case of brief quotations embodied in critical articles and reviews.
First Printing, 2024

CHAPTER 1

Legal Disclaimer

The information contained in this book, "Protecting Our Rights: The Role of First Amendment Auditors," is provided for informational purposes only. While every effort has been made to ensure the accuracy and completeness of the information presented, the authors and publishers make no representations or warranties of any kind, express or implied, about the accuracy, reliability, suitability, or availability with respect to the book or the information, products, services, or related graphics contained in the book for any purpose. Any reliance you place on such information is therefore strictly at your own risk.

The authors and publishers are not engaged in rendering legal, professional, or other advice or services. If legal or other expert assistance is required, the services of a competent professional should be sought. The content of this book is not intended to be a substitute for professional advice, diagnosis, or treatment. Always seek the advice of your attorney or other qualified professional with any questions you may have regarding a legal matter.

The authors and publishers disclaim any liability for any direct, indirect, incidental, consequential, or other damages arising out of or in connection with the use of this book or the information contained herein. This book is sold with the understanding that the authors and publishers are not engaged in rendering legal, professional, or other advice or services.

By using this book, you agree to the terms of this disclaimer. If you do not agree to these terms, please do not use this book.

CHAPTER 2

Introduction

Overview of First Amendment Audits
The concept of First Amendment audits has gained significant attention in recent years, becoming a powerful tool for promoting transparency and accountability in public institutions. But what exactly are First Amendment audits, and why are they so important?

Definition and Purpose

First Amendment audits are activities conducted by individuals, often referred to as auditors, who exercise their right to record in public spaces. These audits are grounded in the First Amendment of the United States Constitution, which guarantees freedoms concerning religion, expression, assembly, and the right to petition. The primary goal of these audits is to ensure that public officials and institutions respect and uphold these constitutional rights.

Auditors typically visit public buildings such as post offices, libraries, courthouses, and police stations, recording their interactions with public employees and officials. By doing so, they test whether these individuals respect the public's right to record and whether they are transparent in their operations. The recordings are often shared on social media platforms, where they can reach a wide audience and spark discussions about civil liberties and government accountability.

Historical Context and Evolution

The practice of First Amendment audits is not new, but it has evolved significantly over time. The roots of this movement can be traced back to the broader civil rights movements of the 1960s and 1970s, when activists used various forms of protest and documentation to highlight injustices and demand change. However, the specific practice of recording public officials to test their adherence to constitutional rights gained prominence in the early 2000s with the rise of digital recording technology and social media.

One of the earliest and most influential figures in the First Amendment audit movement is Philip Turner, also known as "The Battousai." Turner began conducting audits in the mid-2000s, using his camera to document interactions with law enforcement and public officials. His videos, which often highlighted instances of misconduct or ignorance of the law, quickly gained a following and inspired others to take up the cause.

Over the years, the movement has grown, with numerous auditors across the country conducting their own audits and sharing their experiences online. This evolution has been fueled by the increasing accessibility of recording devices and the power of social media to amplify voices and spread information.

Importance of Transparency and Accountability

Transparency and accountability are cornerstones of a healthy democracy. When public institutions operate transparently, they allow citizens to see how decisions are made, how resources are allocated, and how officials conduct themselves. This openness helps to build trust between the public and the government, ensuring that officials are held accountable for their actions.

First Amendment audits play a crucial role in promoting this transparency. By recording interactions with public officials, auditors provide a check on government power, ensuring that officials are acting in accordance with the law and respecting citizens' rights. These recordings can serve as evidence in cases of misconduct, helping to hold officials accountable and drive systemic change.

Moreover, the presence of auditors can act as a deterrent to potential misconduct. When officials know that their actions may be recorded and scrutinized, they are more likely to adhere to proper procedures and treat citizens with respect. This, in turn, fosters a culture of accountability within public institutions.

In conclusion, First Amendment audits are a vital tool for promoting transparency and accountability in public institutions. By exercising their constitutional rights, auditors help to ensure that government officials respect and uphold the freedoms guaranteed by the First Amendment. As the movement continues to grow and evolve, it will undoubtedly play an increasingly important role in safeguarding civil liberties and fostering a more transparent and accountable government.

Personal Motivation

Writing a book about First Amendment audits and the rights to record in public spaces is not just an academic exercise for me; it is a deeply personal endeavor. My journey into this world began with a simple curiosity about our constitutional rights and evolved into a passionate commitment to promoting transparency and accountability in public institutions. In this section, I want to share my personal motivations for writing this book and the experiences that have shaped my perspective.

Why This Book is Important to You

The idea for this book was born out of a growing concern for the erosion of civil liberties and the increasing opacity of public institutions. As I watched news reports and read articles about various incidents where citizens' rights were infringed upon, I felt a strong urge to do something. The more I learned about First Amendment audits, the more I realized their potential to empower ordinary citizens and hold public officials accountable.

This book is important to me because it represents a way to contribute to the ongoing fight for civil liberties. By educating readers about their rights and the importance of transparency, I hope to inspire more people to become active participants in our democracy. The right to record in public spaces is a powerful tool for ensuring that our government remains open and accountable, and I believe that spreading awareness about this right is crucial.

Your Journey and Experiences with First Amendment Audits

My journey into the world of First Amendment audits began with a chance encounter. One day, while browsing through social media, I stumbled upon a video of an auditor conducting an audit at a local post office. The video was both fascinating and eye-opening. It showed the auditor calmly explaining his rights to record in a public space while interacting with postal employees and law enforcement officers. The reactions of the officials ranged from confusion to hostility, but the auditor remained composed and respectful throughout the encounter.

This video sparked my interest, and I began to delve deeper into the world of First Amendment audits. I watched countless videos, read articles and legal documents, and even reached out to some auditors to learn more about their experiences. The more I learned, the more I realized the importance of this movement.

Inspired by what I had seen and learned, I decided to conduct my own audits. My first audit was at a local library, a place I frequented often. Armed with my camera and a solid understanding of my rights, I walked into the library and began recording. The experience was both exhilarating and nerve-wracking. I encountered a mix of reactions from the staff, ranging from curiosity to suspicion. However, by calmly explaining my purpose and my rights, I was able to complete the audit without any major issues.

Over time, I conducted more audits at various public buildings, including post offices, courthouses, and police stations. Each audit was a learning experience, teaching me valuable lessons about the importance of preparation, the need for respectful communication, and the power of persistence. I also encountered challenges, such as confrontations with law enforcement and misunderstandings with public employees. These experiences only strengthened my resolve to continue my work and to share my knowledge with others.

Significant Incidents and Learning Moments

Throughout my journey, there have been several significant incidents that have shaped my perspective and deepened my commitment to First Amendment audits. One such incident occurred during an audit at a local police station. As I was recording the exterior of the building, a police officer approached me and demanded that I stop recording. Despite my attempts to explain my rights, the officer insisted that I was violating the law and threatened to arrest me.

This encounter was a turning point for me. It highlighted the need for better education and awareness about our constitutional rights, both among the public and law enforcement. It also underscored the importance of remaining calm and respectful, even in the face of hostility. I realized that by documenting these interactions and sharing them with others, I could help to promote a better understanding of our rights and the importance of transparency.

How These Experiences Have Shaped Your Perspective

My experiences with First Amendment audits have profoundly shaped my perspective on civil liberties and the role of citizens in holding public institutions accountable. I have come to understand that the right to record in public spaces is not just a legal privilege, but a fundamental aspect of our democracy. It empowers us to be vigilant and active participants in our government, ensuring that those in power remain accountable to the people they serve.

These experiences have also taught me the importance of patience, persistence, and respectful communication. Conducting audits is not always easy, and it often involves navigating complex legal and social dynamics. However, by approaching each audit with a commitment to education and transparency, I have been able to make a positive impact and contribute to the broader movement for civil liberties.

In conclusion, my personal motivation for writing this book is rooted in a deep commitment to promoting transparency and accountability in public institutions. Through my journey and experiences with First Amendment audits, I have gained valuable insights and a renewed sense of purpose. I hope that by sharing my story and the knowledge I have gained, I can inspire others to join the fight for our constitutional rights and help to build a more open and accountable society.

The First Amendment Explained

Understanding the First Amendment is crucial for grasping the significance of First Amendment audits. This foundational element of the United States Constitution guarantees several essential freedoms that form the bedrock of American democracy. In this section, we will delve into the specific freedoms protected by the First Amendment, explore key legal precedents and landmark cases, and discuss their implications for public recording.

Detailed Breakdown of Freedoms

The First Amendment to the United States Constitution is part of the Bill of Rights and reads as follows: "Congress shall make no law respecting an establishment of religion, or prohibiting the free exercise thereof; or abridging the freedom of speech, or of the press; or the right of the people peaceably to assemble, and to petition the Government for a redress of grievances." This single sentence encompasses several distinct freedoms:

1. **Freedom of Speech**: This freedom allows individuals to express themselves without government interference or regulation. It covers a wide range of expressions, including spoken words, written communication, and symbolic actions. For First Amendment auditors, this freedom is fundamental, as it protects their right to speak out and document their interactions with public officials.
2. **Freedom of the Press**: Closely related to freedom of speech, this freedom ensures that the press can operate independently and without censorship. It allows journalists and media organizations to report on government activities and hold public officials accountable. First Amendment auditors often act as citizen journalists, using their recordings to inform the public and promote transparency.
3. **Freedom of Assembly**: This freedom guarantees the right to gather peacefully for demonstrations, protests, and other forms of collective expression. It is essential for auditors who may organize or participate in group audits or public demonstrations to highlight issues of public concern.
4. **Freedom to Petition the Government**: This freedom allows individuals to make their grievances known to the government and seek remedies for injustices. It is a critical tool for

auditors who may use their recordings to advocate for policy changes or legal reforms.

Key Legal Precedents and Landmark Cases
Over the years, numerous court cases have shaped the interpretation and application of the First Amendment. These legal precedents are vital for understanding the rights of First Amendment auditors and the limitations they may encounter. Here are a few landmark cases that have had a significant impact:

1. **New York Times Co. v. United States (1971)**: Also known as the "Pentagon Papers" case, this landmark decision reinforced the principle that the government cannot exercise prior restraint to prevent the publication of classified information unless it can prove a direct, immediate, and irreparable harm to national security. This case underscores the importance of a free press and the public's right to be informed about government actions.
2. **Brandenburg v. Ohio (1969)**: This case established the "imminent lawless action" test, which protects speech advocating for illegal activities unless it is directed to inciting imminent lawless action and is likely to produce such action. This precedent is crucial for auditors, as it protects their right to express dissenting views and criticize public officials without fear of government retaliation.
3. **Glik v. Cunniffe (2011)**: In this case, the First Circuit Court of Appeals ruled that the First Amendment protects the right to record public officials in public spaces. Simon Glik was arrested for recording police officers making an arrest in a public park. The court's decision affirmed that recording public offi-

cials is a form of protected speech, setting a vital precedent for First Amendment auditors.
4. **Turner v. Driver (2017)**: The Fifth Circuit Court of Appeals held that the First Amendment protects the right to record the police. Phillip Turner was detained for recording police officers from a public sidewalk. The court's ruling reinforced the principle that individuals have the right to document public officials performing their duties in public spaces.

Implications for Public Recording

These legal precedents highlight the robust protections afforded by the First Amendment and underscore the importance of public recording as a tool for transparency and accountability. For First Amendment auditors, understanding these rights and the legal landscape is essential for conducting audits effectively and responsibly.

Public recording serves several critical functions:

1. **Promoting Transparency**: By documenting interactions with public officials, auditors help to ensure that government actions are open to public scrutiny. This transparency is vital for maintaining public trust and preventing abuses of power.
2. **Holding Officials Accountable**: Recordings can serve as evidence in cases of misconduct or abuse, helping to hold public officials accountable for their actions. This accountability is crucial for fostering a culture of integrity within public institutions.
3. **Educating the Public**: Auditors' recordings often highlight issues of public concern and educate viewers about their rights. By sharing their experiences, auditors can raise awareness and inspire others to become active participants in the democratic process.

In conclusion, the First Amendment provides a powerful framework for protecting the rights of individuals to express themselves, gather information, and hold their government accountable. For First Amendment auditors, these protections are the foundation of their work, enabling them to promote transparency and accountability through public recording. Understanding the freedoms guaranteed by the First Amendment and the legal precedents that support them is essential for anyone engaged in this important work.

The Role of Auditors

First Amendment auditors play a crucial role in promoting transparency and accountability within public institutions. By exercising their constitutional rights to record in public spaces, these individuals help to ensure that government officials and public employees adhere to the law and respect citizens' rights. In this section, we will explore who First Amendment auditors are, their goals and motivations, and profile some notable auditors who have made significant contributions to the movement.

Who Are First Amendment Auditors?

First Amendment auditors are individuals who conduct audits to test and document the adherence of public officials to constitutional rights, particularly the right to record in public spaces. These auditors come from diverse backgrounds and have varying levels of experience and expertise. Some are seasoned activists with a deep understanding of constitutional law, while others are ordinary citizens who have become passionate about civil liberties.

Despite their differences, all auditors share a common goal: to promote transparency and accountability. They believe that by recording their interactions with public officials, they can highlight instances of misconduct, educate the public about their rights, and encourage government institutions to operate more openly and honestly.

Goals and Motivations

The motivations behind conducting First Amendment audits are as varied as the auditors themselves. However, several common goals unite them:

1. **Promoting Transparency**: Auditors aim to ensure that public institutions operate transparently. By recording their interactions with public officials, they provide a window into the workings of government, allowing the public to see how decisions are made and how officials conduct themselves.
2. **Holding Officials Accountable**: One of the primary motivations for auditors is to hold public officials accountable for their actions. By documenting instances of misconduct or abuse, auditors can provide evidence that may lead to disciplinary action, policy changes, or legal reforms.
3. **Educating the Public**: Many auditors see their work as a form of public education. By sharing their recordings and experiences, they aim to inform citizens about their constitutional rights and the importance of transparency in government. This educational aspect is crucial for empowering individuals to stand up for their rights and participate actively in the democratic process.
4. **Advocating for Change**: Some auditors are motivated by a desire to advocate for broader systemic changes. They use their recordings to highlight issues such as police misconduct, government corruption, or violations of civil liberties, and to push for reforms that address these problems.

Profiles of Notable Auditors

Several auditors have gained prominence within the First Amendment audit community for their impactful work and dedication to promoting transparency and accountability. Here are a few notable figures:

1. **Philip Turner (The Battousai)**: Philip Turner, known by his online alias "The Battousai," is one of the pioneers of the First Amendment audit movement. Turner began conducting audits in the mid-2000s and quickly gained a following for his calm and respectful approach. His videos often highlight instances of law enforcement officers misunderstanding or violating citizens' rights, and his work has inspired many others to take up auditing.
2. **Jeff Gray (HonorYourOath)**: Jeff Gray, who operates under the name "HonorYourOath," is another prominent auditor known for his dedication to civil liberties. Gray's audits often focus on interactions with law enforcement and public officials, and his videos have been instrumental in raising awareness about the importance of respecting constitutional rights. Gray's calm demeanor and thorough knowledge of the law have earned him respect within the auditing community.
3. **James Freeman**: James Freeman is known for his assertive and direct approach to auditing. His videos often feature interactions with law enforcement officers and public officials, and he is not afraid to challenge authority when he believes rights are being violated. Freeman's work has brought attention to numerous instances of misconduct and has sparked important conversations about civil liberties.
4. **News Now Houston (David Warden)**: David Warden, known as "News Now Houston," is a well-known auditor who focuses on recording interactions with law enforcement and public officials in the Houston area. Warden's videos often highlight issues such as police misconduct and govern-

ment transparency, and his work has led to several high-profile legal cases.

Challenges and Criticisms

While First Amendment auditors play a vital role in promoting transparency and accountability, they also face significant challenges and criticisms. Some public officials and members of the public view auditors as disruptive or confrontational, and auditors often encounter hostility or resistance during their audits. Additionally, there are legal and ethical complexities involved in recording public officials, and auditors must navigate these carefully to avoid potential legal repercussions.

Despite these challenges, the work of First Amendment auditors remains crucial for safeguarding civil liberties and ensuring that public institutions operate openly and honestly. By understanding the motivations and goals of auditors, as well as the challenges they face, we can better appreciate the importance of their work and the impact it has on our society.

In conclusion, First Amendment auditors are dedicated individuals who play a vital role in promoting transparency and accountability within public institutions. Through their recordings and interactions with public officials, they help to ensure that government operates in accordance with the law and respects citizens' rights. By highlighting the work of notable auditors and exploring their motivations and challenges, we can gain a deeper understanding of the importance of this movement and the positive impact it has on our society.

Importance of Transparency and Accountability

Transparency and accountability are fundamental principles that underpin a healthy and functioning democracy. They ensure that public institutions operate openly and honestly, fostering trust between the government and its citizens. In this section, we will explore why transparency matters, the role of First Amendment audits in promoting accountability, and the challenges and criticisms faced by auditors.

Why Transparency Matters

Transparency in public institutions is essential for several reasons. First and foremost, it allows citizens to see how decisions are made, how resources are allocated, and how officials conduct themselves. This openness helps to build trust between the public and the government, ensuring that officials are held accountable for their actions.

When public institutions operate transparently, they are more likely to act in the best interests of the public. Transparency helps to prevent corruption, as officials know that their actions are subject to scrutiny. It also encourages better decision-making, as officials are aware that their decisions will be evaluated by the public.

Moreover, transparency empowers citizens by providing them with the information they need to participate actively in the democratic process. When citizens are informed about government actions and policies, they can engage in meaningful discussions, advocate for changes, and hold officials accountable. This active participation is crucial for a vibrant and responsive democracy.

The Role of First Amendment Audits in Promoting Accountability

First Amendment audits play a crucial role in promoting accountability within public institutions. By recording their interactions with public officials, auditors provide a check on government power, ensuring that officials are acting in accordance with the law and respecting citizens' rights. These recordings can serve as evidence in cases of misconduct, helping to hold officials accountable and drive systemic change.

One of the key ways that audits promote accountability is by documenting instances of misconduct or abuse. When auditors record interactions with public officials, they create a permanent record that can be used to highlight issues and advocate for change. For example, if an auditor records a police officer violating a citizen's rights, that recording can be used as evidence in a complaint or legal case. This accountability is crucial for ensuring that public officials are held to high standards of conduct.

Additionally, the presence of auditors can act as a deterrent to potential misconduct. When officials know that their actions may be recorded and scrutinized, they are more likely to adhere to proper procedures and treat citizens with respect. This, in turn, fosters a culture of accountability within public institutions, where officials are aware that they are being watched and held accountable for their actions.

Challenges and Criticisms

While First Amendment audits are essential for promoting transparency and accountability, they are not without challenges and criticisms. Some public officials and members of the public view auditors as disruptive or confrontational, and auditors often encounter hostility or resistance during their audits.

One common criticism is that auditors can be perceived as antagonistic, especially when they challenge officials or refuse to comply with requests to stop recording. This perception can lead to confrontations and escalate tensions, making it difficult for auditors to achieve their goals. To address this, auditors must strive to conduct their audits respectfully and professionally, focusing on education and transparency rather than confrontation.

Another challenge is the legal and ethical complexities involved in recording public officials. While the right to record in public spaces is protected by the First Amendment, there are limitations and nuances that auditors must navigate. For example, certain areas within public buildings may have restrictions on recording for security or privacy reasons. Auditors must be aware of these limitations and ensure that they are conducting their audits within the bounds of the law.

Despite these challenges, the work of First Amendment auditors remains crucial for safeguarding civil liberties and ensuring that public institutions operate openly and honestly. By understanding the criticisms and challenges they face, auditors can develop strategies to overcome these obstacles and continue their important work.

Strategies for Overcoming Challenges

To address the challenges and criticisms they face, First Amendment auditors can adopt several strategies:

1. **Education and Training**: Auditors should educate themselves about their rights and the legal framework surrounding public recording. This knowledge will help them navigate complex situations and respond effectively to challenges.
2. **Respectful Communication**: Auditors should strive to conduct their audits respectfully and professionally. By communicating calmly and clearly, they can reduce tensions and foster positive interactions with public officials.
3. **Building Public Support**: Auditors can build public support by sharing their recordings and experiences with a broader audience. By raising awareness about the importance of transparency and accountability, they can garner support for their work and encourage others to join the movement.
4. **Legal Advocacy**: Auditors should be prepared to advocate for their rights through legal channels if necessary. This may involve filing complaints, seeking legal representation, or par-

ticipating in lawsuits to defend their rights and promote systemic change.

In conclusion, transparency and accountability are essential for a healthy democracy, and First Amendment audits play a crucial role in promoting these principles. By recording their interactions with public officials, auditors help to ensure that government operates openly and honestly, fostering trust and empowering citizens. Despite the challenges and criticisms they face, auditors can adopt strategies to overcome these obstacles and continue their important work. Through their dedication and commitment, First Amendment auditors contribute to a more transparent, accountable, and just society.

CHAPTER 3

Chapter 1: Understanding the First Amendment

Detailed Breakdown of Freedoms

The First Amendment to the United States Constitution is a cornerstone of American democracy, enshrining essential freedoms that protect individual rights and ensure a vibrant, open society. This amendment, part of the Bill of Rights, guarantees several distinct freedoms: speech, press, assembly, and the right to petition the government. Each of these freedoms plays a crucial role in maintaining a democratic society where citizens can express themselves, access information, and hold their government accountable.

Freedom of Speech

Freedom of speech is perhaps the most well-known and fundamental of the First Amendment rights. It allows individuals to express their thoughts, opinions, and beliefs without fear of government censorship or retaliation. This freedom encompasses a wide range of expressions, including spoken words, written communication, and symbolic actions such as protests and demonstrations.

The scope of freedom of speech is broad, protecting not only popular and widely accepted ideas but also controversial and unpopular ones. This protection is vital for fostering a diverse and dynamic public discourse. However, there are limitations to this freedom. Speech that incites imminent lawless action, constitutes true threats, or falls under categories such as obscenity and defamation is not protected by the First Amendment. These exceptions are narrowly defined to balance the need for free expression with the protection of public order and individual rights.

Freedom of the Press

Closely related to freedom of speech, freedom of the press ensures that the media can operate independently and without government interference. This freedom is crucial for a functioning democracy, as it allows journalists and media organizations to investigate, report on, and critique government actions and policies. A free press serves as a watchdog, holding those in power accountable and providing the public with the information they need to make informed decisions.

Historically, freedom of the press has been a driving force behind significant social and political changes. Landmark cases such as New York Times Co. v. United States (1971), also known as the "Pentagon Papers" case, have reinforced the principle that the government cannot exercise prior restraint to prevent the publication of information unless it can prove a direct, immediate, and irreparable harm to national security. This case underscored the importance of a free press in exposing government misconduct and informing the public.

Freedom of Assembly

The right to assemble peacefully is another critical component of the First Amendment. This freedom allows individuals to gather for demonstrations, protests, and other forms of collective expression. It is essential for enabling citizens to come together, share their views, and advocate for change.

Freedom of assembly has played a pivotal role in many social movements throughout American history. From the civil rights marches of the 1960s to contemporary protests advocating for various causes, the ability to assemble peacefully has been a powerful tool for driving social and political change. While this freedom is protected, it is subject to certain regulations to ensure public safety and order. For example, permits may be required for large gatherings, and restrictions may be placed on the time, place, and manner of assemblies.

Freedom to Petition the Government

The right to petition the government for a redress of grievances is a lesser-known but equally important First Amendment freedom. This right allows individuals to make their concerns known to the government and seek remedies for injustices. It encompasses a wide range of activities, from writing letters to government officials to filing lawsuits and organizing petitions.

Historically, the right to petition has been a vital mechanism for citizens to influence government policy and hold officials accountable. It empowers individuals to advocate for changes in laws and policies, ensuring that the government remains responsive to the needs and concerns of its citizens. In modern times, this right continues to be relevant, providing a means for individuals and groups to address issues ranging from local community concerns to national policy debates.

Conclusion

The First Amendment's protections of speech, press, assembly, and petition are foundational to American democracy. These freedoms enable individuals to express themselves, access information, gather for collective action, and seek redress from the government. Understanding these rights is crucial for appreciating the role they play in maintaining a free and open society. For First Amendment auditors, these protections are the bedrock of their work, allowing them to document and challenge government actions, promote transparency, and hold public officials accountable. By exercising and defending these freedoms, auditors contribute to the ongoing effort to safeguard civil liberties and ensure a vibrant, democratic society.

Key Legal Precedents and Landmark Cases

The First Amendment's protections have been shaped and defined by numerous court cases over the years. These legal precedents are crucial for understanding the scope and limitations of First Amendment rights, particularly in the context of public recording and First Amendment audits. In this section, we will explore some of the most significant legal precedents and landmark cases that have influenced First Amendment jurisprudence.

New York Times Co. v. United States (1971)

One of the most pivotal cases in the history of the First Amendment is New York Times Co. v. United States, commonly known as the "Pentagon Papers" case. This landmark decision reinforced the principle that the government cannot exercise prior restraint to prevent the publication of classified information unless it can prove a direct, immediate, and irreparable harm to national security.

In 1971, the New York Times and the Washington Post began publishing excerpts from a classified Department of Defense study detailing the United States' political and military involvement in Vietnam. The Nixon administration sought to prevent further publication, arguing that it posed a threat to national security. The case quickly escalated to the Supreme Court, which ruled in favor of the newspapers. The Court held that the government had not met the heavy burden of proof required to justify prior restraint, thus upholding the First Amendment's protection of a free press.

This case underscored the importance of a free press in exposing government misconduct and informing the public. It set a high bar for government censorship and reinforced the principle that the press must be free to report on matters of public concern without undue interference.

Brandenburg v. Ohio (1969)

Another critical case in First Amendment jurisprudence is Brandenburg v. Ohio, which established the "imminent lawless action" test. This test protects speech advocating for illegal activities unless it is directed to inciting imminent lawless action and is likely to produce such action.

Clarence Brandenburg, a leader of the Ku Klux Klan, was convicted under an Ohio law for advocating violence during a rally. The Supreme Court overturned his conviction, ruling that the government could not punish inflammatory speech unless it was directed to inciting imminent lawless action and was likely to produce such action. This decision significantly expanded the protection of free speech, ensuring that even controversial and offensive speech is protected under the First Amendment.

The Brandenburg test remains a crucial standard for evaluating the limits of free speech, particularly in cases involving advocacy of illegal activities. It underscores the principle that the government cannot suppress speech simply because it is unpopular or provocative.

Glik v. Cunniffe (2011)

Glik v. Cunniffe is a landmark case that affirmed the right to record public officials in public spaces. Simon Glik was arrested for recording police officers making an arrest in a public park in Boston. He was charged with violating the state's wiretap statute, disturbing the peace, and aiding in the escape of a prisoner.

Glik filed a lawsuit, arguing that his First Amendment rights had been violated. The First Circuit Court of Appeals ruled in his favor, stating that the First Amendment protects the right to record public officials in public spaces. The court emphasized that recording public officials is a form of protected speech, as it contributes to the public's ability to hold government accountable.

This decision was a significant victory for First Amendment auditors and citizen journalists, reinforcing the principle that individuals have the right to document public officials performing their duties in public spaces.

Turner v. Driver (2017)

Turner v. Driver is another important case that reinforced the right to record police officers. Phillip Turner was detained for recording police officers from a public sidewalk in Fort Worth, Texas. He filed a lawsuit, arguing that his First Amendment rights had been violated.

The Fifth Circuit Court of Appeals ruled in Turner's favor, holding that the First Amendment protects the right to record the police. The court stated that the right to record public officials, including police officers, is clearly established and that individuals have the right to document public officials performing their duties in public spaces.

This ruling further solidified the legal protections for recording public officials and provided important guidance for law enforcement agencies on respecting citizens' First Amendment rights.

Other Relevant Cases

In addition to these landmark cases, several other legal precedents have shaped First Amendment rights. For example, cases such as Tinker v. Des Moines Independent Community School District (1969) and Texas v. Johnson (1989) have reinforced the protection of symbolic speech, while cases like Citizens United v. Federal Election Commission (2010) have expanded the scope of free speech in the context of political spending.

These cases collectively underscore the robust protections afforded by the First Amendment and highlight the importance of understanding the legal landscape for First Amendment auditors. By familiarizing themselves with these precedents, auditors can better navigate the complexities of public recording and advocate for their rights effectively.

In conclusion, key legal precedents and landmark cases have played a crucial role in defining and protecting First Amendment rights. From the Pentagon Papers case to the right to record public officials, these decisions have reinforced the principles of free speech, press, assembly, and petition. For First Amendment auditors, understanding these legal precedents is essential for conducting audits effectively and responsibly, ensuring that their work contributes to a more transparent and accountable society.

The Role of First Amendment Auditors

First Amendment auditors play a pivotal role in promoting transparency and accountability within public institutions. By exercising their constitutional rights to record in public spaces, these individuals help ensure that government officials and public employees adhere to the law and respect citizens' rights. In this section, we will explore who First Amendment auditors are, their goals and motivations, their methods and approaches, and the challenges and criticisms they face.

Who Are First Amendment Auditors?

First Amendment auditors are individuals who conduct audits to test and document the adherence of public officials to constitutional rights, particularly the right to record in public spaces. These auditors come from diverse backgrounds and have varying levels of experience and expertise. Some are seasoned activists with a deep understanding of constitutional law, while others are ordinary citizens who have become passionate about civil liberties.

Despite their differences, all auditors share a common goal: to promote transparency and accountability. They believe that by recording their interactions with public officials, they can highlight instances of misconduct, educate the public about their rights, and encourage government institutions to operate more openly and honestly.

Goals and Motivations

The motivations behind conducting First Amendment audits are as varied as the auditors themselves. However, several common goals unite them:

1. **Promoting Transparency**: Auditors aim to ensure that public institutions operate transparently. By recording their interactions with public officials, they provide a window into the workings of government, allowing the public to see how decisions are made and how officials conduct themselves.
2. **Holding Officials Accountable**: One of the primary motivations for auditors is to hold public officials accountable for their actions. By documenting instances of misconduct or abuse, auditors can provide evidence that may lead to disciplinary action, policy changes, or legal reforms.
3. **Educating the Public**: Many auditors see their work as a form of public education. By sharing their recordings and experiences, they aim to inform citizens about their constitutional rights and the importance of transparency in government. This educational aspect is crucial for empowering individuals to stand up for their rights and participate actively in the democratic process.

4. **Advocating for Change**: Some auditors are motivated by a desire to advocate for broader systemic changes. They use their recordings to highlight issues such as police misconduct, government corruption, or violations of civil liberties, and to push for reforms that address these problems.

Methods and Approaches

First Amendment auditors employ a variety of methods and approaches to conduct their audits. While their techniques may differ, several common practices are widely used:

1. **Recording Public Officials**: Auditors typically visit public buildings such as post offices, libraries, courthouses, and police stations, recording their interactions with public employees and officials. They often focus on areas where the public has a right to be present, ensuring that their activities are within legal boundaries.
2. **Engaging with Officials**: During their audits, auditors may engage with public officials to test their knowledge of constitutional rights and their willingness to respect those rights. This can involve asking questions, requesting information, or simply observing how officials respond to being recorded.
3. **Documenting and Sharing**: Auditors document their experiences through video recordings, which they often share on social media platforms. This allows them to reach a wide audience and raise awareness about their findings. The recordings can also serve as evidence in cases of misconduct or legal disputes.
4. **Remaining Respectful and Professional**: While some auditors may adopt a more confrontational approach, many strive to conduct their audits respectfully and professionally.

They aim to educate rather than provoke, focusing on promoting transparency and accountability through constructive engagement.

Challenges and Criticisms

While First Amendment auditors play a vital role in promoting transparency and accountability, they also face significant challenges and criticisms. Some public officials and members of the public view auditors as disruptive or confrontational, and auditors often encounter hostility or resistance during their audits.

One common criticism is that auditors can be perceived as antagonistic, especially when they challenge officials or refuse to comply with requests to stop recording. This perception can lead to confrontations and escalate tensions, making it difficult for auditors to achieve their goals. To address this, auditors must strive to conduct their audits respectfully and professionally, focusing on education and transparency rather than confrontation.

Another challenge is the legal and ethical complexities involved in recording public officials. While the right to record in public spaces is protected by the First Amendment, there are limitations and nuances that auditors must navigate. For example, certain areas within public buildings may have restrictions on recording for security or privacy reasons. Auditors must be aware of these limitations and ensure that they are conducting their audits within the bounds of the law.

Despite these challenges, the work of First Amendment auditors remains crucial for safeguarding civil liberties and ensuring that public institutions operate openly and honestly. By understanding the criticisms and challenges they face, auditors can develop strategies to overcome these obstacles and continue their important work.

Strategies for Overcoming Challenges

To address the challenges and criticisms they face, First Amendment auditors can adopt several strategies:

1. **Education and Training**: Auditors should educate themselves about their rights and the legal framework surrounding public recording. This knowledge will help them navigate complex situations and respond effectively to challenges.
2. **Respectful Communication**: Auditors should strive to conduct their audits respectfully and professionally. By communicating calmly and clearly, they can reduce tensions and foster positive interactions with public officials.
3. **Building Public Support**: Auditors can build public support by sharing their recordings and experiences with a broader audience. By raising awareness about the importance of transparency and accountability, they can garner support for their work and encourage others to join the movement.
4. **Legal Advocacy**: Auditors should be prepared to advocate for their rights through legal channels if necessary. This may involve filing complaints, seeking legal representation, or participating in lawsuits to defend their rights and promote systemic change.

In conclusion, First Amendment auditors are dedicated individuals who play a vital role in promoting transparency and accountability within public institutions. Through their recordings and interactions with public officials, they help to ensure that government operates in accordance with the law and respects citizens' rights. By understanding the motivations and goals of auditors, as well as the challenges they face, we can better appreciate the importance of their work and the impact it has on our society.

The Impact of First Amendment Audits

First Amendment audits have a profound impact on promoting transparency, holding officials accountable, educating the public, and building a culture of accountability within public institutions. By exercising their constitutional rights to record in public spaces, auditors play a crucial role in ensuring that government actions are open to scrutiny and that officials are held responsible for their conduct. In this section, we will explore the various ways in which First Amendment audits make a significant difference.

Promoting Transparency

Transparency is a cornerstone of democratic governance. When public institutions operate transparently, they allow citizens to see how decisions are made, how resources are allocated, and how officials conduct themselves. First Amendment audits are instrumental in promoting this transparency.

Auditors visit public buildings such as post offices, libraries, courthouses, and police stations, recording their interactions with public employees and officials. These recordings provide a window into the workings of government, allowing the public to observe how officials respond to inquiries, handle public interactions, and adhere to legal and ethical standards. By documenting these interactions, auditors help to ensure that government actions are open to public scrutiny.

For example, an audit at a local police station might reveal how officers handle public inquiries, respond to complaints, or conduct routine operations. If the audit uncovers instances of misconduct or non-compliance with the law, it can prompt internal reviews, policy changes, or disciplinary actions. This transparency helps to build public trust and ensures that officials are accountable for their actions.

Holding Officials Accountable

One of the primary motivations for First Amendment auditors is to hold public officials accountable for their actions. By documenting instances of misconduct or abuse, auditors provide evidence that can lead to disciplinary action, policy changes, or legal reforms.

Case studies of successful audits highlight the impact of this accountability. For instance, an auditor might record a public official engaging in discriminatory behavior or violating a citizen's rights. The recording can be used as evidence in a complaint or legal case, leading to disciplinary action against the official and changes in institutional policies to prevent future misconduct.

In another example, an audit at a public health department might uncover issues such as inadequate service, lack of transparency in decision-making, or failure to follow proper procedures. The documentation provided by the auditor can prompt investigations, reforms, and improvements in service delivery, ultimately benefiting the public.

Educating the Public

First Amendment audits also serve an important educational function. By sharing their recordings and experiences, auditors inform citizens about their constitutional rights and the importance of transparency in government. This educational aspect is crucial for empowering individuals to stand up for their rights and participate actively in the democratic process.

Auditors often use social media platforms to share their recordings, reaching a wide audience and sparking discussions about civil liberties and government accountability. These recordings can highlight issues such as police misconduct, government corruption, or violations of civil liberties, raising awareness and prompting public debate.

For example, an auditor might share a video of an interaction with a public official who attempts to prevent recording in a public space. The video can educate viewers about their right to record in public areas and the legal protections afforded by the First Amendment. By raising awareness about these rights, auditors empower citizens to exercise their freedoms and hold officials accountable.

Building a Culture of Accountability

The long-term impact of First Amendment audits extends beyond individual cases of misconduct. By promoting transparency and accountability, auditors contribute to building a culture of accountability within public institutions. This culture is characterized by a commitment to openness, ethical behavior, and responsiveness to public concerns.

When public officials know that their actions may be recorded and scrutinized, they are more likely to adhere to proper procedures and treat citizens with respect. This deterrent effect helps to prevent misconduct and fosters a culture of integrity within public institutions.

Moreover, the presence of auditors can encourage public institutions to adopt proactive measures to promote transparency and accountability. For example, a police department might implement body-worn cameras, establish clear policies for public interactions, or provide training on constitutional rights. These measures can enhance public trust and ensure that officials are held to high standards of conduct.

Conclusion

In conclusion, First Amendment audits have a significant impact on promoting transparency, holding officials accountable, educating the public, and building a culture of accountability within public institutions. By exercising their constitutional rights to record in public spaces, auditors play a crucial role in ensuring that government actions are open to scrutiny and that officials are held responsible for their conduct. Through their dedication and commitment, First

Amendment auditors contribute to a more transparent, accountable, and just society. Their work underscores the importance of safeguarding civil liberties and fostering a vibrant, democratic society where citizens can actively participate and hold their government accountable.

Future Trends and Emerging Issues

As society evolves, so too do the challenges and opportunities related to First Amendment rights. The landscape of public recording and First Amendment audits is continually shaped by technological advancements, legal developments, social and political contexts, and the evolving role of auditors. In this section, we will explore these future trends and emerging issues, providing insights into how they may impact the practice of First Amendment audits.

Technological Advancements

Technology has always played a crucial role in the exercise of First Amendment rights, and recent advancements continue to transform the landscape of public recording. The proliferation of smartphones with high-quality cameras has made it easier than ever for individuals to document their interactions with public officials. Additionally, the rise of social media platforms has provided auditors with powerful tools to share their recordings and reach a global audience.

Looking ahead, several technological trends are likely to impact First Amendment audits:

1. **Body-Worn Cameras**: Many law enforcement agencies are adopting body-worn cameras to increase transparency and accountability. These devices can provide an additional layer of documentation, complementing the recordings made by auditors. However, the use of body-worn cameras also raises questions about privacy, data storage, and access to footage.

2. **Live Streaming**: The ability to live stream audits in real-time is becoming increasingly popular. Platforms like Facebook Live, YouTube, and Instagram allow auditors to broadcast their interactions as they happen, providing immediate transparency and reducing the risk of footage being tampered with or lost.
3. **Drones and Wearable Technology**: Emerging technologies such as drones and wearable cameras offer new possibilities for documenting public spaces and interactions. These tools can provide unique perspectives and enhance the ability of auditors to capture comprehensive footage.

While these technological advancements offer significant benefits, they also present challenges. Issues related to privacy, data security, and the potential for misuse of technology must be carefully navigated to ensure that the rights of all individuals are respected.

Legal Developments

The legal landscape surrounding First Amendment rights is continually evolving, with ongoing debates and potential changes that could impact the practice of First Amendment audits. Several key legal developments are worth noting:

1. **Legislation on Public Recording**: Some states have introduced or are considering legislation that affects the right to record in public spaces. These laws may impose restrictions or provide additional protections for auditors. It is essential for auditors to stay informed about these legal changes and understand how they impact their rights and responsibilities.
2. **Court Rulings**: Future court rulings will continue to shape the interpretation and application of First Amendment rights. Cases involving public recording, police accountability,

and free speech are likely to set important precedents that will influence the practice of First Amendment audits.
3. **Privacy Laws**: As concerns about privacy grow, new laws and regulations may be introduced to address issues related to recording in public spaces. Auditors must be aware of these developments and ensure that their practices comply with evolving legal standards.

Social and Political Context

The social and political context in which First Amendment audits take place can significantly influence their practice and impact. Several factors are likely to shape the future of First Amendment audits:

1. **Public Perception**: The way the public perceives First Amendment audits can affect their effectiveness and acceptance. Efforts to educate the public about the importance of transparency and accountability can help build support for auditors and their work.
2. **Political Climate**: Changes in the political climate, including shifts in government policies and leadership, can impact the environment in which auditors operate. Supportive policies and leadership can enhance the effectiveness of audits, while restrictive measures can pose challenges.
3. **Social Movements**: Social movements advocating for civil liberties, police reform, and government transparency can influence the practice of First Amendment audits. These movements can provide support, resources, and a broader context for auditors' work.

The Evolving Role of Auditors

As the landscape of First Amendment rights continues to evolve, so too does the role of auditors. Several trends are likely to shape the future of First Amendment audits:

1. **Professionalization**: As the practice of auditing becomes more widespread, there may be a move towards greater professionalization. This could include the development of best practices, training programs, and professional organizations to support auditors.
2. **Collaboration**: Auditors may increasingly collaborate with other civil liberties organizations, journalists, and community groups to amplify their impact. These partnerships can provide additional resources, expertise, and support for auditors' work.
3. **Advocacy and Policy Change**: Auditors may take on a more active role in advocating for policy changes and legal reforms. By using their recordings and experiences to highlight systemic issues, auditors can contribute to broader efforts to promote transparency and accountability.

Conclusion

In conclusion, the future of First Amendment audits is shaped by a dynamic interplay of technological advancements, legal developments, social and political contexts, and the evolving role of auditors. As these trends and issues continue to unfold, auditors must remain adaptable and informed, leveraging new tools and strategies to promote transparency and accountability. By staying engaged with these emerging trends, First Amendment auditors can continue to play a vital role in safeguarding civil liberties and ensuring a vibrant, democratic society. Through their dedication and commitment, auditors contribute to a more open and accountable government, empowering citizens to exercise their rights and hold public officials accountable.

CHAPTER 4

Chapter 2: Public Buildings and Spaces

Types of Public Buildings

Public buildings are essential spaces where citizens interact with government services and officials. These buildings, funded by taxpayer dollars, are generally open to the public and serve various functions, from providing essential services to maintaining public order. Understanding the types of public buildings and the legal rights to record within them is crucial for First Amendment auditors. This section explores several key types of public buildings, highlighting the legal rights to record, notable incidents, and case studies.

Post Offices

Post offices are ubiquitous public buildings that provide essential mail services to the community. As federal facilities, they are subject to specific regulations regarding public access and recording. The United States Postal Service (USPS) has guidelines that allow for recording in publicly accessible areas, such as lobbies, foyers, and corridors, as long as it does not disrupt operations or violate privacy.

Notable incidents involving audits at post offices often revolve around misunderstandings of these guidelines. For example, an auditor might record in a post office lobby, only to be confronted by staff who are unaware of the public's right to record. These encounters can serve as educational moments, both for the staff and the public, highlighting the importance of understanding and respecting First Amendment rights.

Department of Motor Vehicles (DMV) and Bureau of Motor Vehicles (BMV)

DMVs and BMVs are state-run facilities that handle vehicle registration, driver licensing, and other related services. These buildings are often busy and can be stressful environments for both employees and visitors. Recording in DMVs and BMVs is generally allowed in public areas, but auditors must be mindful of not disrupting operations or infringing on individuals' privacy.

Examples of audits in DMVs and BMVs often involve interactions with security personnel or staff who may not be familiar with the legal rights to record. Successful audits in these settings can lead to increased awareness and better training for employees, ensuring that they respect the public's right to record while maintaining order and privacy.

Health Departments

Health departments provide a range of public health services, from immunizations to health education and inspections. These facilities often deal with sensitive information and vulnerable populations, making privacy a significant concern. While recording in public areas of health departments is generally permitted, auditors must be particularly careful to avoid capturing private health information or disrupting services.

Case studies of audits in health departments highlight the delicate balance between transparency and privacy. For instance, an auditor might record in a health department lobby to document public interactions but must ensure that no private conversations or sensitive information are captured. These audits can raise important discussions about the need for transparency in public health services while respecting individual privacy.

Libraries

Libraries are public spaces that provide access to information, resources, and community programs. They are often seen as bastions of free speech and intellectual freedom. Recording in libraries is typically allowed in public areas, such as reading rooms and common spaces, but auditors must be mindful of library policies and the need for a quiet environment.

Notable incidents in libraries often involve interactions with staff who may be concerned about privacy or disruption. For example, an auditor might record a public meeting or event in a library, only to be questioned by staff about their intentions. These encounters can serve as opportunities to educate both staff and patrons about the importance of transparency and the public's right to record in these spaces.

Courthouses

Courthouses are critical public buildings where legal proceedings take place. Recording in courthouses is subject to strict regulations to ensure the integrity of the judicial process and protect the privacy of individuals involved in legal matters. While public areas such as lobbies and exteriors may be recorded, courtrooms and certain restricted areas typically have prohibitions on recording.

High-profile cases involving audits in courthouses often revolve around the tension between transparency and the need to maintain order and privacy in legal proceedings. For example, an auditor might record outside a courtroom to document public access and interactions but must respect the rules prohibiting recording inside the courtroom. These audits can highlight the importance of transparency in the judicial system while respecting the legal constraints that protect the integrity of legal proceedings.

Probation Offices

Probation offices are public facilities where individuals on probation meet with their probation officers and receive various services. These offices often deal with sensitive information and individuals in vulnerable situations, making privacy a significant concern. Recording in public areas of probation offices is generally allowed, but auditors must be careful to avoid capturing private conversations or sensitive information.

Case studies of audits in probation offices often involve interactions with staff who may be concerned about privacy and security. For example, an auditor might record in a probation office lobby to document public interactions but must ensure that no private conversations or sensitive information are captured. These audits can raise important discussions about the need for transparency in probation services while respecting individual privacy.

Police Stations

Police stations are public buildings where law enforcement officers work and interact with the community. Recording in police stations is generally allowed in public areas, such as lobbies and exteriors, but auditors must be mindful of security concerns and privacy issues. Interactions with law enforcement officers can be particularly challenging, as officers may have varying levels of understanding about the public's right to record.

Legal precedents and notable audits in police stations often highlight the importance of transparency and accountability in law enforcement. For example, an auditor might record in a police station lobby to document public interactions and ensure that officers respect citizens' rights. These audits can lead to increased awareness and better training for law enforcement officers, ensuring that they respect the public's right to record while maintaining security and order.

In conclusion, understanding the types of public buildings and the legal rights to record within them is crucial for First Amendment auditors. By conducting audits in these settings, auditors promote transparency, hold officials accountable, and educate the public about their rights. Each type of public building presents unique challenges and opportunities, and successful audits can lead to positive changes and increased awareness of First Amendment rights.

Legal Rights to Record

Understanding the legal rights to record in public buildings is essential for First Amendment auditors. These rights are grounded in federal and state laws, which provide the framework for what is permissible when recording in public spaces. This section delves into the relevant laws, notable case studies, common challenges auditors face, and strategies for navigating restrictions.

Federal and State Laws

The right to record in public spaces is primarily protected under the First Amendment, which guarantees freedoms of speech and press. This protection extends to recording public officials and activities in public areas. However, the specifics can vary based on federal and state laws.

At the federal level, the First Amendment provides a broad protection for recording in public spaces. This includes areas such as lobbies, foyers, and corridors of public buildings. The Department of Homeland Security (DHS) has issued guidelines affirming that photography and recording in publicly accessible areas of federal buildings are generally permitted, provided it does not interfere with operations or security.

State laws can vary significantly, with some states offering more explicit protections for recording in public spaces. For example, states like California and New York have robust protections for recording public officials, while others may have more restrictive laws. It is crucial for auditors to familiarize themselves with the specific laws in their state to ensure they are operating within legal boundaries.

Case Studies and Examples

Several notable legal cases have reinforced the right to record in public spaces, providing important precedents for auditors:

1. **Glik v. Cunniffe (2011)**: This landmark case involved Simon Glik, who was arrested for recording police officers making an arrest in a public park. The First Circuit Court of Appeals ruled in Glik's favor, affirming that the First Amendment protects the right to record public officials in public spaces. This case set a crucial precedent for auditors, reinforcing their right to document public interactions.
2. **Turner v. Driver (2017)**: Phillip Turner was detained for recording police officers from a public sidewalk in Fort Worth, Texas. The Fifth Circuit Court of Appeals ruled that the First Amendment protects the right to record the police, further solidifying the legal protections for auditors.
3. **Smith v. City of Cumming (2000)**: In this case, the Eleventh Circuit Court of Appeals held that individuals have a First Amendment right to record matters of public interest, including police activities. This decision reinforced the principle that recording public officials is a protected form of speech.

These cases highlight the importance of legal precedents in protecting the rights of auditors and ensuring that public officials respect these rights.

Common Challenges

Despite the legal protections, auditors often face challenges when recording in public buildings. These challenges can include:

1. **Misunderstanding of the Law**: Public officials and employees may not be fully aware of the legal rights to record, leading to confrontations and attempts to stop auditors from recording. Educating officials and the public about these rights is crucial for reducing conflicts.
2. **Hostility and Intimidation**: Auditors may encounter hostility or intimidation from public officials or security personnel. It is essential for auditors to remain calm and assertive, clearly explaining their rights and the legal basis for their actions.
3. **Legal Pushback**: In some cases, auditors may face legal pushback, including arrests or citations for recording in public spaces. Understanding the legal framework and having access to legal support can help auditors navigate these challenges.

Navigating Restrictions

While recording in public areas of public buildings is generally permitted, there are certain restrictions that auditors must be aware of:

1. **Restricted Areas**: Some areas within public buildings, such as secure zones or areas with sensitive information, may have restrictions on recording. Auditors should respect these restrictions and focus on publicly accessible areas.
2. **Interference with Operations**: Recording should not interfere with the normal operations of public buildings. Auditors

should be mindful of not disrupting services or obstructing employees in the performance of their duties.
3. **Privacy Concerns**: Auditors must be careful not to capture private conversations or sensitive information, particularly in areas like health departments or probation offices. Balancing transparency with respect for privacy is crucial.

Strategies for Overcoming Challenges

To effectively navigate the legal landscape and overcome challenges, auditors can adopt several strategies:

1. **Education and Preparation**: Auditors should educate themselves about the relevant federal and state laws, as well as any specific policies of the public buildings they plan to audit. Being well-prepared can help auditors assert their rights confidently.
2. **Clear Communication**: When confronted, auditors should communicate clearly and respectfully, explaining their rights and the legal basis for their actions. Providing printed copies of relevant laws or court rulings can be helpful.
3. **Legal Support**: Having access to legal support, such as attorneys or legal advocacy organizations, can provide auditors with the resources they need to defend their rights and address any legal challenges that arise.
4. **Documentation**: Auditors should document their interactions thoroughly, including recording any confrontations or attempts to stop them from recording. This documentation can serve as evidence in legal disputes and help protect their rights.

In conclusion, understanding the legal rights to record in public buildings is essential for First Amendment auditors. By familiarizing themselves with federal and state laws, learning from notable case studies, and adopting effective strategies, auditors can navigate the legal landscape and promote transparency and accountability in public institutions. Despite the challenges, the legal protections for recording in public spaces provide a strong foundation for auditors to exercise their rights and contribute to a more open and accountable government.

Privacy Concerns and Ethical Considerations

First Amendment audits, while essential for promoting transparency and accountability, must be conducted with a keen awareness of privacy concerns and ethical considerations. Balancing the public's right to know with individuals' rights to privacy is a delicate task that requires auditors to navigate complex legal and ethical landscapes. This section explores the concept of reasonable expectation of privacy, strategies for balancing transparency and privacy, case studies of privacy conflicts, and best practices for auditors.

Reasonable Expectation of Privacy

The concept of reasonable expectation of privacy is a cornerstone of privacy law. It refers to the idea that individuals have a right to privacy in situations where they can reasonably expect it. This expectation varies depending on the context and location. For example, individuals generally have a high expectation of privacy in their homes but a lower expectation in public spaces.

In the context of First Amendment audits, understanding reasonable expectation of privacy is crucial. Public buildings, by their nature, are places where individuals may have limited expectations of privacy, especially in common areas like lobbies, hallways, and public meeting rooms. However, certain areas within public buildings, such as restrooms, private offices, and areas where sensitive information is handled, may have higher expectations of privacy.

Auditors must be aware of these distinctions and ensure that their activities do not infringe on individuals' privacy rights. Recording in public areas is generally permissible, but auditors should avoid capturing private conversations or sensitive information.

Balancing Transparency and Privacy

Balancing the need for transparency with respect for privacy is a key ethical consideration for First Amendment auditors. While the goal of audits is to promote openness and accountability, this should not come at the expense of individuals' privacy rights. Auditors must navigate this balance carefully to maintain the integrity of their work and uphold ethical standards.

Several strategies can help auditors achieve this balance:

1. **Awareness and Sensitivity**: Auditors should be aware of the privacy implications of their actions and be sensitive to the context in which they are recording. This includes recognizing areas where individuals may have a higher expectation of privacy and avoiding recording in those areas.
2. **Clear Communication**: When conducting audits, auditors should communicate clearly with public officials and individuals present. Explaining the purpose of the audit and the legal basis for recording can help alleviate concerns and foster cooperation.
3. **Selective Recording**: Auditors can focus their recording on interactions with public officials and avoid capturing private conversations or sensitive information. This selective approach helps to respect individuals' privacy while still promoting transparency.

4. **Ethical Decision-Making**: Auditors should consider the ethical implications of their actions and make decisions that prioritize respect for privacy. This includes being mindful of the potential impact of their recordings on individuals and the broader community.

Case Studies of Privacy Conflicts

Examining case studies of privacy conflicts can provide valuable insights into the challenges auditors face and how they can be resolved. Here are a few examples:

1. **Health Department Audit**: An auditor records in the lobby of a health department, capturing interactions with public officials. However, the recording inadvertently captures a private conversation between two individuals discussing sensitive health information. The auditor recognizes the privacy concern and decides to edit the recording to remove the private conversation before sharing it publicly. This approach respects privacy while still promoting transparency.
2. **Library Audit**: During an audit in a public library, the auditor records a public meeting. A library staff member expresses concern that the recording might capture private conversations between patrons. The auditor addresses the concern by focusing the camera on the public meeting and avoiding areas where private conversations are likely to occur. This selective recording approach helps to balance transparency with privacy.
3. **Police Station Audit**: An auditor records in the lobby of a police station, documenting interactions with officers. A police officer asks the auditor to stop recording, citing concerns about capturing private information related to ongoing inves-

tigations. The auditor explains their legal right to record in public areas but agrees to avoid recording any sensitive information. This compromise respects privacy while upholding the auditor's rights.

Best Practices for Auditors

To conduct audits ethically and responsibly, auditors should follow best practices that prioritize respect for privacy while promoting transparency:

1. **Research and Preparation**: Auditors should research the specific public buildings they plan to audit and understand any relevant policies or restrictions. Being well-prepared helps auditors navigate privacy concerns effectively.
2. **Respectful Engagement**: Auditors should engage respectfully with public officials and individuals present during audits. Clear communication and a respectful demeanor can help build trust and cooperation.
3. **Mindful Recording**: Auditors should be mindful of what they are recording and avoid capturing private conversations or sensitive information. Focusing on interactions with public officials and public activities helps to maintain ethical standards.
4. **Editing and Sharing**: Before sharing recordings publicly, auditors should review and edit their footage to remove any content that may infringe on individuals' privacy. This careful review process ensures that the recordings promote transparency without compromising privacy.
5. **Continuous Learning**: Auditors should stay informed about legal developments, privacy laws, and ethical guidelines related to public recording. Continuous learning helps audi-

tors adapt to changing contexts and uphold high ethical standards.

In conclusion, privacy concerns and ethical considerations are critical aspects of First Amendment audits. By understanding reasonable expectation of privacy, balancing transparency with respect for privacy, learning from case studies, and following best practices, auditors can conduct their work responsibly and ethically. This approach ensures that audits promote transparency and accountability while respecting individuals' privacy rights, contributing to a more open and just society.

Practical Tips for Conducting Audits

Conducting First Amendment audits requires careful preparation, respectful engagement, and a thorough understanding of legal rights and best practices. This section provides practical tips for auditors, covering preparation and research, conducting the audit, dealing with law enforcement, and documenting and sharing audits. By following these guidelines, auditors can ensure their activities are effective, respectful, and legally sound.

Preparation and Research

Effective audits begin with thorough preparation and research. Understanding the legal landscape and specific policies of the public buildings you plan to audit is crucial for a successful and conflict-free experience.

1. **Know the Laws**: Familiarize yourself with federal, state, and local laws regarding public recording. This includes understanding your rights under the First Amendment and any specific regulations that apply to the buildings you plan to audit. Knowledge of relevant court cases, such as Glik v. Cunniffe and Turner v. Driver, can also be beneficial.

2. **Research the Location**: Before conducting an audit, research the specific public building. Understand its layout, public access areas, and any posted policies regarding recording. This information can help you navigate the building more effectively and avoid areas with restrictions.
3. **Plan Your Approach**: Decide on the specific areas you want to audit and the interactions you aim to document. Having a clear plan can help you stay focused and organized during the audit.
4. **Prepare Your Equipment**: Ensure your recording equipment is in good working order. This includes checking your camera or smartphone, ensuring you have sufficient battery life and storage space, and having any necessary accessories, such as tripods or external microphones.

Conducting the Audit

When conducting the audit, it is essential to remain respectful, professional, and aware of your surroundings. The goal is to promote transparency and accountability without causing unnecessary disruptions.

1. **Introduce Yourself**: When you enter the public building, introduce yourself to any staff or security personnel you encounter. Explain that you are conducting a First Amendment audit and briefly outline your rights to record in public areas. This can help set a positive tone and reduce misunderstandings.
2. **Stay Calm and Respectful**: Maintain a calm and respectful demeanor throughout the audit. If you encounter resistance or hostility, respond politely and assertively, explaining your

legal rights. Avoid escalating confrontations and remain focused on your objective.
3. **Focus on Public Areas**: Conduct your audit in publicly accessible areas, such as lobbies, hallways, and public meeting rooms. Avoid restricted areas or spaces where individuals have a reasonable expectation of privacy, such as private offices or restrooms.
4. **Document Interactions**: Record your interactions with public officials and employees, focusing on how they respond to your presence and your right to record. Be mindful of capturing clear audio and video to ensure your documentation is effective.

Dealing with Law Enforcement

Interactions with law enforcement can be one of the most challenging aspects of First Amendment audits. Understanding your rights and knowing how to handle these interactions is crucial.

1. **Know Your Rights**: Be well-versed in your legal rights to record in public spaces. This includes understanding the protections provided by the First Amendment and any relevant state laws. Familiarize yourself with key court rulings that support your right to record.
2. **Stay Composed**: If approached by law enforcement, remain calm and composed. Clearly explain that you are conducting a First Amendment audit and outline your legal rights. Provide any relevant documentation or court rulings if necessary.
3. **Comply with Lawful Orders**: While you have the right to record, it is essential to comply with lawful orders from law enforcement officers. If an officer instructs you to move to a

different area or stop recording in a restricted space, comply respectfully while asserting your rights.
4. **Document the Interaction**: Record your interaction with law enforcement, ensuring you capture clear audio and video. This documentation can be valuable if you need to address any legal challenges or complaints.

Documenting and Sharing Audits

Effective documentation and sharing of your audits are crucial for promoting transparency and accountability. Follow these tips to ensure your recordings are impactful and reach a broad audience.

1. **Review and Edit Footage**: After completing your audit, review your recordings to ensure they are clear and accurate. Edit the footage to remove any private conversations or sensitive information that may have been inadvertently captured.
2. **Provide Context**: When sharing your recordings, provide context for your audience. Explain the purpose of the audit, the location, and any relevant legal information. This helps viewers understand the significance of your findings.
3. **Choose the Right Platforms**: Share your recordings on platforms that reach a broad audience and support your goals. Social media platforms like YouTube, Facebook, and Instagram are popular choices for auditors. Consider creating a dedicated channel or page for your audits to build a following and engage with your audience.
4. **Engage with Your Audience**: Encourage viewers to share your recordings and engage in discussions about the importance of transparency and accountability. Respond to comments and questions to foster a sense of community and support for your work.

5. **Maintain Professionalism**: When sharing your recordings, maintain a professional tone and focus on the facts. Avoid inflammatory language or personal attacks, as this can undermine the credibility of your work.

In conclusion, conducting First Amendment audits requires careful preparation, respectful engagement, and effective documentation. By following these practical tips, auditors can ensure their activities are impactful, legally sound, and contribute to promoting transparency and accountability in public institutions. Through their dedication and commitment, auditors play a vital role in safeguarding civil liberties and fostering a more open and just society.

Positive Outcomes and Success Stories

First Amendment audits have led to numerous positive outcomes, demonstrating the power of transparency and accountability in public institutions. By documenting their interactions with public officials and sharing their findings, auditors have inspired changes in policies, improved public awareness, and fostered a culture of accountability. This section highlights examples of successful audits, their impact on public institutions, the long-term effects of audits, and stories of individuals inspired to take action.

Examples of Successful Audits

Successful audits often result in tangible changes that enhance transparency and accountability. Here are a few notable examples:

1. **Police Station Audit**: An auditor conducted an audit at a local police station, recording interactions with officers and documenting their responses to public inquiries. The audit revealed instances of officers providing incorrect information about citizens' rights to record. The video gained significant attention online, prompting the police department to review

its training procedures. As a result, the department implemented new training programs to ensure officers were well-informed about First Amendment rights, leading to improved interactions with the public.
2. **DMV Audit**: During an audit at a Department of Motor Vehicles (DMV) office, an auditor recorded staff members who were unaware of the public's right to record in the facility. The video highlighted the need for better staff training on legal rights and public access. Following the audit, the DMV conducted a comprehensive review of its policies and provided additional training to employees, ensuring they understood and respected citizens' rights to record in public areas.
3. **Library Audit**: An auditor recorded a public meeting at a library, documenting the proceedings and interactions with library staff. The audit revealed that the library had unclear policies regarding public recording. The video sparked a community discussion about transparency and access to public meetings. In response, the library updated its policies to explicitly allow recording of public meetings, promoting greater transparency and public engagement.

Impact on Public Institutions

First Amendment audits have a significant impact on public institutions, leading to increased transparency, accountability, and improved public trust. By documenting and sharing their findings, auditors highlight areas where institutions can improve and encourage positive changes.

1. **Policy Changes**: Audits often prompt public institutions to review and update their policies to ensure they align with legal standards and respect citizens' rights. For example, a health

department might revise its policies to clarify public access and recording rights, ensuring that staff are well-informed and prepared to handle interactions with auditors.
2. **Training and Education**: Successful audits can lead to improved training and education for public employees. Institutions may implement new training programs to ensure staff understand their legal obligations and the rights of the public. This can result in more informed and respectful interactions between public officials and citizens.
3. **Increased Accountability**: By documenting instances of misconduct or non-compliance, audits hold public officials accountable for their actions. This accountability can lead to disciplinary actions, policy reforms, and a greater emphasis on ethical behavior within public institutions.

Building a Culture of Accountability

The long-term effects of First Amendment audits extend beyond individual cases, contributing to a broader culture of accountability within public institutions. This culture is characterized by a commitment to transparency, ethical behavior, and responsiveness to public concerns.

1. **Deterrence of Misconduct**: The presence of auditors and the potential for public scrutiny can deter misconduct and encourage public officials to adhere to proper procedures. Knowing that their actions may be recorded and shared publicly, officials are more likely to act in accordance with the law and treat citizens with respect.
2. **Proactive Measures**: Public institutions may adopt proactive measures to promote transparency and accountability. For example, a police department might implement body-worn

cameras, establish clear policies for public interactions, or provide regular training on constitutional rights. These measures can enhance public trust and ensure that officials are held to high standards of conduct.
3. **Community Engagement**: Audits can foster greater community engagement by raising awareness about citizens' rights and encouraging public participation in government activities. By highlighting issues of public concern, audits can inspire individuals to become more involved in their communities and advocate for positive changes.

Inspiring Others

First Amendment audits have inspired many individuals to take action and become more engaged in promoting transparency and accountability. Stories of successful audits and their impact can motivate others to conduct their own audits, advocate for policy changes, or support efforts to protect civil liberties.

1. **New Auditors**: Many individuals are inspired to become auditors themselves after witnessing the positive impact of successful audits. They see the power of documenting public interactions and holding officials accountable, and they want to contribute to the movement for transparency and accountability.
2. **Community Activism**: Audits can inspire broader community activism, encouraging individuals to advocate for policy changes, participate in public meetings, or support organizations that promote civil liberties. This activism can lead to meaningful changes and a more engaged and informed public.

3. **Educational Impact**: By sharing their recordings and experiences, auditors educate the public about their rights and the importance of transparency. This educational impact can empower individuals to stand up for their rights, engage in informed discussions, and hold public officials accountable.

In conclusion, First Amendment audits have led to numerous positive outcomes, demonstrating the power of transparency and accountability in public institutions. Successful audits have prompted policy changes, improved training and education, and fostered a culture of accountability. By inspiring others to take action and promoting greater community engagement, auditors contribute to a more open and just society. Their dedication and commitment to safeguarding civil liberties ensure that public institutions operate transparently and ethically, benefiting the entire community.

CHAPTER 5

Chapter 3: The Fourth Amendment and Privacy Concer

The Fourth Amendment Explained

The Fourth Amendment to the United States Constitution is a critical component of the Bill of Rights, providing essential protections against unreasonable searches and seizures. This amendment plays a vital role in safeguarding individual privacy and ensuring that government actions are conducted within the bounds of the law. In this section, we will explore the scope and significance of the Fourth Amendment, key legal precedents and landmark cases, and its application in modern contexts.

Protection Against Unreasonable Searches and Seizures

The Fourth Amendment states: "The right of the people to be secure in their persons, houses, papers, and effects, against unreasonable searches and seizures, shall not be violated, and no Warrants shall issue, but upon probable cause, supported by Oath or affirmation, and particularly describing the place to be searched, and the persons or things to be seized." This amendment provides a fundamental protection for individuals against arbitrary and intrusive actions by the government.

The scope of the Fourth Amendment is broad, covering various forms of searches and seizures, including physical searches of property, electronic surveillance, and the collection of personal data. The key principle underlying the Fourth Amendment is reasonableness. Searches and seizures must be reasonable, and in most cases, this requires a warrant issued by a judge based on probable cause. The warrant must specify the place to be searched and the items to be seized, ensuring that government actions are not overly broad or invasive.

Historical Context and the Framers' Intent

The Fourth Amendment was born out of the historical context of the American colonies' experience with British rule. Colonists were subjected to arbitrary searches and seizures by British authorities, who used general warrants and writs of assistance to search homes and businesses without specific cause. These practices were deeply resented and viewed as violations of personal liberty and property rights.

The framers of the Constitution sought to prevent such abuses by establishing clear protections against unreasonable searches and seizures. The Fourth Amendment reflects their intent to create a legal framework that balances the need for law enforcement with the protection of individual privacy. By requiring warrants based on probable cause, the framers aimed to ensure that government actions were justified and limited in scope.

Key Legal Principles and Protections

Several key legal principles and protections have emerged from the interpretation of the Fourth Amendment:

1. **Probable Cause**: For a search or seizure to be reasonable, it must be based on probable cause. This means that there must be a reasonable basis to believe that a crime has been commit-

ted and that evidence of the crime will be found in the place to be searched.
2. **Warrants**: In most cases, a warrant is required for a search or seizure to be lawful. The warrant must be issued by a neutral judge or magistrate and must specify the place to be searched and the items to be seized.
3. **Exclusionary Rule**: Evidence obtained in violation of the Fourth Amendment is generally inadmissible in court. This principle, known as the exclusionary rule, serves as a deterrent against unlawful searches and seizures by law enforcement.
4. **Reasonable Expectation of Privacy**: The Fourth Amendment protects individuals in situations where they have a reasonable expectation of privacy. This principle has been applied to various contexts, including homes, vehicles, and electronic communications.

Legal Precedents and Landmark Cases

Several landmark cases have shaped the interpretation and application of the Fourth Amendment:

1. **Mapp v. Ohio (1961)**: This case established the exclusionary rule at the state level, holding that evidence obtained in violation of the Fourth Amendment cannot be used in state courts. The decision reinforced the importance of protecting individual rights against unlawful searches and seizures.
2. **Katz v. United States (1967)**: In this case, the Supreme Court expanded the scope of the Fourth Amendment to include electronic surveillance. The Court held that the Fourth Amendment protects individuals' reasonable expectation of privacy, even in public spaces. This decision set a precedent for the protection of privacy in the digital age.

3. **Terry v. Ohio (1968)**: This case addressed the issue of stop-and-frisk procedures. The Supreme Court ruled that law enforcement officers can stop and frisk individuals based on reasonable suspicion, a lower standard than probable cause. This decision balanced the need for effective policing with the protection of individual rights.

Application in Modern Contexts

The Fourth Amendment continues to be highly relevant in modern contexts, particularly with the advent of digital technology and surveillance. Issues such as electronic surveillance, data collection, and the use of advanced technologies by law enforcement present new challenges for interpreting the Fourth Amendment.

1. **Digital Privacy**: The rise of digital communication and data storage has raised questions about the application of the Fourth Amendment to electronic surveillance and data collection. Courts have grappled with issues such as the legality of warrantless searches of cell phones, email accounts, and other digital devices.
2. **Surveillance Technologies**: The use of surveillance technologies, such as drones, facial recognition, and GPS tracking, has prompted debates about the balance between security and privacy. Courts have had to consider whether the use of these technologies constitutes a search under the Fourth Amendment and whether warrants are required.
3. **Data Collection**: Government agencies' collection of personal data, such as metadata from phone records and internet activity, has raised concerns about mass surveillance and the potential for abuse. Legal challenges have focused on whether

such practices violate the Fourth Amendment's protections against unreasonable searches and seizures.

In conclusion, the Fourth Amendment provides essential protections against unreasonable searches and seizures, safeguarding individual privacy and ensuring that government actions are conducted within the bounds of the law. Understanding the historical context, key legal principles, and landmark cases is crucial for appreciating the significance of the Fourth Amendment. As technology continues to evolve, the application of the Fourth Amendment to modern contexts presents new challenges and opportunities for protecting individual rights in the digital age.

Balancing Privacy and Transparency

Balancing privacy and transparency is a fundamental challenge in a democratic society. Both principles are essential for ensuring individual freedoms and maintaining public trust in government institutions. This section explores the role of privacy in a democratic society, the importance of transparency and accountability, and strategies for finding the right balance between these two crucial values.

The Role of Privacy in a Democratic Society

Privacy is a cornerstone of individual freedom and autonomy. It allows people to control their personal information, make independent decisions, and engage in private activities without undue interference. In a democratic society, privacy supports several key functions:

1. **Personal Autonomy**: Privacy enables individuals to make choices about their lives, relationships, and activities without external pressure or surveillance. This autonomy is essential for personal development and self-expression.

2. **Freedom of Thought and Expression**: Privacy protects the space for individuals to think, explore ideas, and express themselves freely. Without privacy, people may feel inhibited or fearful of expressing dissenting or unpopular views.
3. **Protection from Abuse of Power**: Privacy acts as a safeguard against the misuse of power by government and other entities. It prevents unwarranted intrusions into individuals' lives and ensures that personal information is not exploited for malicious purposes.
4. **Civic Engagement**: Privacy fosters a sense of security and trust, encouraging individuals to participate in civic activities, engage in public discourse, and advocate for their rights. When people feel their privacy is protected, they are more likely to engage actively in democratic processes.

Transparency and Accountability

Transparency is equally vital for a functioning democracy. It ensures that government actions are open to scrutiny, allowing citizens to hold public officials accountable and make informed decisions. Transparency promotes several key benefits:

1. **Accountability**: Transparent government operations enable citizens to monitor and evaluate the actions of public officials. This accountability helps prevent corruption, abuse of power, and misconduct.
2. **Public Trust**: Transparency builds trust between the government and the public. When citizens have access to information about government activities, they are more likely to trust that officials are acting in their best interests.
3. **Informed Decision-Making**: Access to information allows citizens to make informed decisions about policies, elections,

and other civic matters. Transparency ensures that the public is well-informed and can engage meaningfully in democratic processes.
4. **Efficiency and Effectiveness**: Transparent operations can lead to more efficient and effective government. When actions are open to scrutiny, officials are incentivized to perform their duties competently and ethically.

Finding the Balance

Balancing privacy and transparency requires careful consideration of the context and the interests at stake. Strategies for achieving this balance include:

1. **Contextual Sensitivity**: Recognize that the balance between privacy and transparency may vary depending on the context. For example, transparency is crucial in government decision-making processes, while privacy is paramount in personal health information.
2. **Clear Policies and Guidelines**: Establish clear policies and guidelines that outline the boundaries of privacy and transparency. These policies should be based on legal standards and ethical principles, providing a framework for decision-making.
3. **Stakeholder Engagement**: Involve stakeholders, including the public, in discussions about privacy and transparency. Engaging diverse perspectives can help identify potential conflicts and develop solutions that respect both values.
4. **Proportionality and Necessity**: Ensure that measures to promote transparency are proportionate and necessary. For example, public access to government records should be bal-

anced with the need to protect sensitive information that could harm individuals or national security.
5. **Education and Awareness**: Educate public officials and citizens about the importance of both privacy and transparency. Awareness campaigns can help build a shared understanding of these values and promote responsible practices.

Case Studies and Examples of Successful Balance

Examining case studies where privacy and transparency have been successfully balanced can provide valuable insights and lessons:

1. **Public Health Reporting**: During public health crises, such as the COVID-19 pandemic, transparency about infection rates and government responses is crucial. However, protecting individuals' health information is equally important. Successful strategies have included anonymizing data and providing aggregated information to inform the public while safeguarding privacy.
2. **Police Body-Worn Cameras**: The use of body-worn cameras by police officers is an example of balancing transparency and privacy. These cameras promote accountability by documenting interactions between officers and the public. However, policies must ensure that recordings do not infringe on individuals' privacy rights, such as by restricting access to footage and protecting sensitive information.
3. **Government Transparency Initiatives**: Many governments have implemented transparency initiatives, such as open data portals, to provide public access to information. These initiatives often include safeguards to protect personal data and sensitive information, ensuring that transparency does not compromise privacy.

In conclusion, balancing privacy and transparency is essential for maintaining individual freedoms and public trust in a democratic society. Privacy protects personal autonomy and freedom, while transparency ensures accountability and informed decision-making. By adopting strategies that consider context, establish clear policies, engage stakeholders, and promote education, it is possible to achieve a balance that respects both values. Examining successful case studies can provide valuable lessons and guide efforts to navigate the complex interplay between privacy and transparency. Through thoughtful and responsible practices, we can ensure that both privacy and transparency are upheld, contributing to a more open, just, and democratic society.

Navigating Privacy Concerns in Specific Public Buildings

Conducting First Amendment audits in specific public buildings presents unique challenges, particularly when it comes to respecting privacy. Each type of public building has its own set of privacy concerns and legal considerations that auditors must navigate carefully. This section explores privacy issues and best practices for conducting audits in health departments, courthouses, probation offices, libraries, and other public buildings.

Health Departments

Health departments provide a range of public health services, often dealing with sensitive personal information. Privacy concerns in these settings are paramount, as they involve individuals' health records and personal data. Auditors must be particularly cautious to avoid capturing any private health information during their audits.

1. **Privacy Concerns**: Health departments handle confidential health information protected by laws such as the Health Insurance Portability and Accountability Act (HIPAA). Auditors must ensure that their recordings do not capture private

conversations or documents containing personal health information.
2. **Strategies for Conducting Audits**: To respect privacy while promoting transparency, auditors should focus on public areas such as lobbies and waiting rooms. They should avoid recording in areas where private health information is likely to be discussed or displayed. If an auditor inadvertently captures sensitive information, they should edit the footage to remove any private content before sharing it publicly.
3. **Case Studies**: In one case, an auditor conducted an audit in a health department lobby, documenting interactions with public officials. The auditor was careful to avoid recording any private conversations or health records. The audit highlighted the importance of transparency in public health services while respecting individuals' privacy.

Courthouses

Courthouses are critical public buildings where legal proceedings take place. Balancing transparency with the need for confidentiality in legal proceedings is a significant challenge in these settings. Legal restrictions on recording in courthouses are often stringent to protect the integrity of the judicial process and the privacy of individuals involved.

1. **Balancing Transparency and Confidentiality**: While transparency in the judicial system is essential, it must be balanced with the need to protect the privacy of individuals involved in legal proceedings. This includes witnesses, jurors, and defendants.
2. **Legal Restrictions**: Recording inside courtrooms is generally prohibited to maintain the integrity of legal proceedings

and protect the privacy of participants. However, recording in public areas such as lobbies and exteriors of courthouses is typically allowed. Auditors must be aware of and comply with these restrictions.
3. **Case Studies**: An auditor conducted an audit outside a courthouse, documenting public access and interactions with security personnel. The auditor respected the prohibition on recording inside the courtroom, focusing instead on public areas. This approach ensured that the audit promoted transparency without compromising the confidentiality of legal proceedings.

Probation Offices

Probation offices deal with individuals on probation, often involving sensitive information and vulnerable populations. Privacy concerns in these settings are significant, and auditors must navigate these concerns carefully to avoid infringing on individuals' privacy rights.

1. **Privacy Issues**: Probation offices handle confidential information about individuals' legal status, personal history, and compliance with probation terms. Auditors must ensure that their recordings do not capture private conversations or documents containing sensitive information.
2. **Best Practices**: Auditors should focus on public areas such as lobbies and waiting rooms, avoiding areas where private conversations or sensitive information are likely to be discussed. If an auditor inadvertently captures private information, they should edit the footage to remove any sensitive content before sharing it publicly.

3. **Case Studies**: In one instance, an auditor conducted an audit in a probation office lobby, documenting interactions with public officials. The auditor was careful to avoid recording any private conversations or documents. The audit highlighted the importance of transparency in probation services while respecting individuals' privacy.

Libraries and Other Public Buildings

Libraries and other public buildings, such as community centers and government offices, also present unique privacy concerns. These spaces often serve as community hubs, providing access to information and services while respecting individuals' privacy.

1. **Privacy Considerations**: Libraries and similar public buildings may host private meetings, provide access to sensitive information, or serve vulnerable populations. Auditors must be mindful of these privacy concerns when conducting audits.
2. **Best Practices**: Auditors should focus on public areas such as reading rooms, common spaces, and public meeting rooms. They should avoid recording private meetings or capturing sensitive information. Clear communication with staff and patrons about the purpose of the audit can help alleviate privacy concerns.
3. **Case Studies**: An auditor conducted an audit in a public library, documenting a public meeting and interactions with library staff. The auditor respected the privacy of patrons by avoiding areas where private conversations were likely to occur. The audit promoted transparency in library operations while respecting individuals' privacy.

Conclusion

Navigating privacy concerns in specific public buildings is a critical aspect of conducting First Amendment audits. By understanding the unique privacy issues in health departments, courthouses, probation offices, libraries, and other public buildings, auditors can conduct their work responsibly and ethically. Focusing on public areas, avoiding sensitive information, and respecting legal restrictions are essential strategies for balancing transparency and privacy. Through careful and respectful auditing practices, auditors can promote transparency and accountability while safeguarding individuals' privacy rights. This approach ensures that audits contribute to a more open and just society, where public institutions operate transparently and ethically.

Ethical Considerations for Auditors

Conducting First Amendment audits requires a strong ethical foundation to ensure that the rights of individuals are respected while promoting transparency and accountability. Ethical considerations are crucial for maintaining public trust and conducting audits responsibly. This section explores the importance of respecting privacy while promoting transparency, handling sensitive information, building trust with the public, and provides case studies of ethical auditing practices.

Respecting Privacy While Promoting Transparency

Balancing the need for transparency with respect for privacy is a fundamental ethical consideration for auditors. While the goal of audits is to promote openness and accountability, this should not come at the expense of individuals' privacy rights. Auditors must navigate this balance carefully to maintain the integrity of their work and uphold ethical standards.

1. **Ethical Guidelines for Auditors**: Auditors should adhere to ethical guidelines that prioritize respect for privacy. This in-

cludes avoiding the recording of private conversations, sensitive information, or areas where individuals have a reasonable expectation of privacy. Ethical guidelines help ensure that audits are conducted responsibly and respectfully.

2. **Strategies for Minimizing Privacy Intrusions**: Auditors can adopt strategies to minimize privacy intrusions while conducting audits. This includes focusing on public areas, using selective recording techniques, and being mindful of the context in which they are recording. By taking these precautions, auditors can promote transparency without compromising privacy.

Handling Sensitive Information

Auditors may encounter sensitive or private information during their audits. Handling this information responsibly is crucial for maintaining ethical standards and protecting individuals' privacy rights.

1. **Best Practices for Dealing with Sensitive Information**: Auditors should take steps to ensure that sensitive information is not inadvertently captured or shared. This includes reviewing and editing recordings to remove any private content before sharing them publicly. Auditors should also be aware of legal requirements for handling sensitive information, such as data protection laws.
2. **Legal and Ethical Responsibilities**: Auditors have both legal and ethical responsibilities when it comes to handling sensitive information. They must comply with relevant laws and regulations, such as data protection and privacy laws, and adhere to ethical principles that prioritize respect for individuals' privacy.

Building Trust with the Public

Trust is a critical component of effective auditing. Building and maintaining public trust requires auditors to conduct their work transparently, ethically, and respectfully.

1. **Importance of Trust in Conducting Effective Audits**: Trust is essential for gaining public support and cooperation during audits. When the public trusts that auditors are acting ethically and responsibly, they are more likely to support and engage with the auditing process.
2. **Ways to Build and Maintain Public Trust**: Auditors can build and maintain public trust by being transparent about their intentions, communicating clearly with the public, and adhering to ethical guidelines. Engaging with the community, responding to concerns, and demonstrating a commitment to ethical practices are also important for building trust.

Case Studies of Ethical Auditing

Examining case studies of ethical auditing practices can provide valuable insights and lessons for auditors. These examples highlight how auditors can balance transparency and privacy while conducting their work responsibly.

1. **Health Department Audit**: An auditor conducted an audit in a health department lobby, documenting interactions with public officials. The auditor was careful to avoid recording any private conversations or health records. By focusing on public areas and respecting privacy, the auditor promoted transparency while maintaining ethical standards.
2. **Library Audit**: During an audit in a public library, the auditor recorded a public meeting and interactions with library

staff. The auditor respected the privacy of patrons by avoiding areas where private conversations were likely to occur. This approach ensured that the audit promoted transparency without compromising individuals' privacy.

3. **Police Station Audit**: An auditor recorded in the lobby of a police station, documenting interactions with officers. The auditor communicated clearly with the officers, explaining the purpose of the audit and their legal rights. By maintaining a respectful and professional demeanor, the auditor built trust and conducted the audit ethically.

Conclusion

Ethical considerations are paramount for First Amendment auditors. By respecting privacy while promoting transparency, handling sensitive information responsibly, and building trust with the public, auditors can conduct their work ethically and effectively. Adhering to ethical guidelines, adopting strategies to minimize privacy intrusions, and learning from case studies of ethical auditing practices are essential for maintaining the integrity of audits. Through their dedication to ethical standards, auditors contribute to a more transparent, accountable, and just society, ensuring that public institutions operate openly and respect individuals' rights.

CHAPTER 6

Chapter 4: Recording Private Businesses from Publi

Legal Framework

Recording private businesses from public sidewalks is a practice that intersects with several legal principles, primarily rooted in the First Amendment's protection of free speech and press. Understanding the legal framework that governs this activity is crucial for auditors to conduct their work effectively and responsibly. This section explores the legal rights to record from public sidewalks, key legal precedents, and the limitations and restrictions that auditors must navigate.

Rights to Record from Public Sidewalks

The right to record from public sidewalks is generally protected under the First Amendment, which guarantees freedoms of speech and press. Public sidewalks are considered traditional public forums, where individuals have broad rights to express themselves and document their surroundings. This includes recording anything that is visible from the public space, such as the exterior of private businesses.

The distinction between public and private property is fundamental in this context. Public sidewalks are owned and maintained by the government, making them accessible to the public for various activities, including recording. In contrast, private property, such as the interior of a business, is subject to the property owner's rules and restrictions. Auditors must remain on public sidewalks to ensure they are within their legal rights.

Relevant Federal and State Laws

While the First Amendment provides a broad protection for recording in public spaces, specific federal and state laws can influence the practice. For example, federal laws generally support the right to record in public forums, but state laws may vary in their application and interpretation.

Some states have enacted laws that explicitly protect the right to record public officials and activities in public spaces. These laws reinforce the First Amendment protections and provide additional legal backing for auditors. However, other states may have more restrictive laws that limit recording in certain contexts or impose additional requirements, such as obtaining consent from individuals being recorded.

Auditors must familiarize themselves with the specific laws in their state to ensure they are operating within legal boundaries. Understanding both federal and state laws is essential for navigating the complexities of recording private businesses from public sidewalks.

Key Legal Precedents

Several significant court cases have defined and reinforced the right to record from public sidewalks. These legal precedents provide important guidance for auditors and help clarify the scope of their rights.

1. **Glik v. Cunniffe (2011)**: This landmark case involved Simon Glik, who was arrested for recording police officers making an arrest in a public park. The First Circuit Court of Appeals ruled in Glik's favor, affirming that the First Amendment protects the right to record public officials in public spaces. This case set a crucial precedent for auditors, reinforcing their right to document public interactions from public sidewalks.
2. **Turner v. Driver (2017)**: Phillip Turner was detained for recording police officers from a public sidewalk in Fort Worth, Texas. The Fifth Circuit Court of Appeals ruled that the First Amendment protects the right to record the police, further solidifying the legal protections for auditors. This ruling emphasized that public sidewalks are traditional public forums where individuals have broad rights to record.
3. **Smith v. City of Cumming (2000)**: In this case, the Eleventh Circuit Court of Appeals held that individuals have a First Amendment right to record matters of public interest, including police activities. This decision reinforced the principle that recording public officials from public sidewalks is a protected form of speech.

These cases highlight the importance of legal precedents in protecting the rights of auditors and ensuring that public officials respect these rights. By understanding these precedents, auditors can better navigate legal challenges and assert their rights confidently.

Limitations and Restrictions

While the right to record from public sidewalks is broadly protected, there are limitations and restrictions that auditors must be aware of. These limitations are designed to balance the rights of individuals with the need to maintain public order and respect privacy.

1. **Harassment and Stalking Laws**: Auditors must ensure that their recording activities do not cross the line into harassment or stalking. Persistent or aggressive recording that targets specific individuals or businesses may be subject to legal action under harassment or stalking laws.
2. **Reasonable Expectation of Privacy**: While recording from public sidewalks is generally permissible, auditors must be mindful of individuals' reasonable expectation of privacy. For example, recording through the windows of a private business into areas where individuals have a reasonable expectation of privacy, such as restrooms or private offices, may be legally problematic.
3. **Obstruction and Trespassing**: Auditors must avoid obstructing pedestrian traffic or trespassing onto private property. Staying on public sidewalks and ensuring that recording activities do not interfere with the normal use of the space is essential for maintaining legal compliance.
4. **Local Ordinances**: Some municipalities may have local ordinances that impose additional restrictions on recording activities. Auditors should research and understand any local regulations that may apply to their activities.

In conclusion, the legal framework governing the recording of private businesses from public sidewalks is rooted in the First Amendment's protections of free speech and press. Understanding the rights to record, key legal precedents, and the limitations and restrictions is crucial for auditors to conduct their work effectively and responsibly. By staying informed and adhering to legal guidelines, auditors can promote transparency and accountability while respecting the rights of individuals and businesses.

Ethical Considerations and Best Practices

Recording private businesses from public sidewalks involves navigating a complex landscape of ethical considerations. While the legal right to record from public spaces is generally protected, auditors must balance this right with respect for privacy and the potential impact on business owners and employees. This section explores the ethical considerations when recording private businesses, best practices for auditors, and strategies for engaging with business owners and employees.

Respecting Privacy

Respecting privacy is a fundamental ethical consideration for auditors. While public sidewalks are traditional public forums where recording is generally permissible, auditors must be mindful of the privacy rights of individuals and businesses.

1. **Ethical Considerations When Recording Private Businesses**: Auditors should consider the potential impact of their recordings on the privacy of individuals and businesses. This includes being aware of areas where individuals have a reasonable expectation of privacy, such as inside private offices or through windows into private spaces. Recording in a manner that respects these privacy boundaries is crucial for maintaining ethical standards.
2. **Balancing the Right to Record with Respect for Privacy**: Auditors must strike a balance between exercising their right to record and respecting the privacy of individuals and businesses. This involves being selective about what is recorded and ensuring that the focus remains on public interactions and activities. Avoiding intrusive or invasive recording practices helps maintain this balance.

Best Practices for Auditors

Adopting best practices is essential for conducting audits ethically and effectively. These guidelines help auditors navigate the complexities of recording private businesses from public sidewalks while minimizing conflicts and respecting privacy.

1. **Guidelines for Conducting Audits Ethically**: Auditors should follow ethical guidelines that prioritize respect for privacy and responsible recording practices. This includes avoiding recording private conversations, sensitive information, or areas where individuals have a reasonable expectation of privacy. Ethical guidelines help ensure that audits are conducted responsibly and respectfully.
2. **Tips for Minimizing Conflicts and Respecting Privacy**: To minimize conflicts and respect privacy, auditors should:
    - Focus on public areas and interactions that are visible from the public sidewalk.
    - Avoid recording through windows or into private spaces where individuals have a reasonable expectation of privacy.
    - Clearly communicate the purpose of the audit to business owners and employees, explaining the legal basis for recording.
    - Be prepared to address concerns and answer questions from business owners and employees in a respectful and informative manner.

Engaging with Business Owners and Employees

Effective communication with business owners and employees is crucial for conducting audits smoothly and ethically. Building positive relationships and addressing concerns can help mitigate conflicts and foster understanding.

1. **Strategies for Communicating with Business Owners and Employees**: Auditors should approach interactions with business owners and employees with respect and transparency. This includes:
    - Introducing themselves and explaining the purpose of the audit.
    - Providing information about the legal rights to record from public sidewalks.
    - Addressing any concerns or questions in a calm and respectful manner.
    - Being open to dialogue and willing to listen to the perspectives of business owners and employees.
2. **Handling Confrontations and Misunderstandings**: Confrontations and misunderstandings can arise during audits, particularly if business owners or employees are unaware of the legal rights to record. To handle these situations effectively, auditors should:
    - Remain calm and composed, avoiding escalation.
    - Clearly explain the legal basis for recording and provide relevant information or documentation if necessary.
    - Respectfully address any concerns and seek to find common ground.
    - If the situation becomes hostile or unmanageable, consider disengaging and seeking legal advice or support.

Case Studies of Ethical Auditing

Examining case studies of ethical auditing practices can provide valuable insights and lessons for auditors. These examples highlight how auditors can balance transparency and privacy while conducting their work responsibly.

1. **Retail Store Audit**: An auditor conducted an audit outside a retail store, documenting interactions with customers and employees. The auditor focused on public areas and avoided recording through windows or into private spaces. By clearly communicating the purpose of the audit and addressing any concerns respectfully, the auditor was able to conduct the audit ethically and effectively.
2. **Restaurant Audit**: During an audit outside a restaurant, the auditor recorded interactions with patrons and staff. The auditor introduced themselves to the restaurant manager and explained the purpose of the audit. By maintaining a respectful and professional demeanor, the auditor built trust and conducted the audit without conflicts.
3. **Office Building Audit**: An auditor recorded outside an office building, documenting public interactions and activities. The auditor avoided recording through windows or into private offices, focusing instead on the exterior and public areas. By respecting privacy boundaries and communicating clearly with building staff, the auditor conducted the audit ethically and responsibly.

Conclusion

Ethical considerations are paramount for auditors recording private businesses from public sidewalks. By respecting privacy, adopting best practices, and engaging effectively with business owners and employees, auditors can conduct their work ethically and responsibly. Following ethical guidelines, minimizing conflicts, and learning from case studies of ethical auditing practices are essential for maintaining the integrity of audits. Through their dedication to ethical standards, auditors contribute to a more transparent, accountable, and just society, ensuring that public interactions and activities are documented responsibly and respectfully.

Challenges and Controversies

Recording private businesses from public sidewalks can be fraught with challenges and controversies. While the legal right to record from public spaces is generally protected, auditors often face conflicts, legal challenges, and varying public perceptions. This section explores common conflicts, potential legal issues, and strategies for addressing these challenges, as well as the public perception of recording private businesses.

Common Conflicts

Auditors frequently encounter conflicts when recording private businesses from public sidewalks. These conflicts can arise from misunderstandings, resistance from business owners and employees, or concerns about privacy and disruption.

1. **Misunderstandings About Legal Rights**: Many conflicts stem from misunderstandings about the legal rights to record from public sidewalks. Business owners and employees may not be aware that public sidewalks are traditional public forums where recording is generally permissible. This lack of awareness can lead to confrontations and attempts to stop auditors from recording.
2. **Resistance from Business Owners and Employees**: Business owners and employees may resist being recorded due to concerns about privacy, security, or potential negative publicity. This resistance can manifest as verbal confrontations, demands to stop recording, or even physical attempts to block the camera.
3. **Concerns About Privacy and Disruption**: Recording activities can raise concerns about privacy and disruption, par-

ticularly if auditors are perceived as intrusive or disruptive to business operations. Customers and employees may feel uncomfortable being recorded, leading to complaints and conflicts.

Examples of Disputes and Resolutions
Examining examples of disputes and how they were resolved can provide valuable insights for auditors. These case studies highlight effective strategies for addressing conflicts and maintaining ethical standards.

1. **Retail Store Dispute**: An auditor recording outside a retail store was confronted by the store manager, who demanded that the recording stop. The auditor calmly explained their legal right to record from the public sidewalk and provided information about relevant laws. The manager, initially resistant, eventually understood the auditor's rights and allowed the recording to continue. This resolution was achieved through clear communication and a respectful approach.
2. **Restaurant Confrontation**: During an audit outside a restaurant, the auditor was approached by an employee who expressed concerns about privacy and disruption. The auditor addressed these concerns by explaining the purpose of the audit and ensuring that the recording focused on public interactions and did not capture private conversations. The employee's concerns were alleviated, and the audit proceeded without further conflict.
3. **Office Building Conflict**: An auditor recording outside an office building faced resistance from security personnel, who attempted to block the camera and demanded that the recording stop. The auditor remained calm and asserted their legal

right to record from the public sidewalk. The situation was resolved when the auditor provided documentation of relevant legal precedents, convincing the security personnel to allow the recording to continue.

Legal Challenges

Auditors may encounter legal challenges when recording private businesses from public sidewalks. Understanding potential legal issues and strategies for addressing them is crucial for protecting auditors' rights.

1. **Potential Legal Issues**: Legal challenges can arise from accusations of harassment, stalking, or trespassing. Business owners may file complaints or seek legal action against auditors, claiming that the recording activities are intrusive or disruptive.
2. **Strategies for Defending Rights in Court**: To defend their rights in court, auditors should:
   - Document all interactions and recording activities thoroughly, including video evidence and written notes.
   - Familiarize themselves with relevant legal precedents and laws that protect the right to record from public sidewalks.
   - Seek legal representation or support from civil liberties organizations if faced with legal action.
   - Present clear and compelling evidence that their recording activities were conducted lawfully and ethically.

Public Perception

Public perception of recording private businesses can vary widely. While some individuals support transparency and accountability, others may view recording activities as intrusive or unnecessary.

1. **How the Public Perceives Recording Private Businesses**: Public perception can be influenced by factors such as the context of the recording, the behavior of the auditor, and the nature of the business being recorded. Positive perceptions are more likely when auditors conduct their activities respectfully and transparently.
2. **Strategies for Improving Public Understanding and Support**: To improve public understanding and support, auditors can:
    - Clearly communicate the purpose and importance of their audits, emphasizing the role of transparency and accountability.
    - Engage with the community and address any concerns or questions from the public.
    - Share positive outcomes and success stories from previous audits to demonstrate the benefits of recording activities.
    - Maintain a respectful and professional demeanor during audits, fostering trust and credibility.

Conclusion

Recording private businesses from public sidewalks presents a range of challenges and controversies. By understanding common conflicts, potential legal issues, and public perceptions, auditors can navigate these challenges effectively. Clear communication, respectful engagement, and thorough documentation are essential strategies for addressing conflicts and defending legal rights. By promoting transparency and accountability while respecting privacy and public concerns, auditors can conduct their work ethically and responsibly, contributing to a more open and just society. Through their dedication and commitment, auditors help ensure that public interactions and activities are documented responsibly and transparently.

Case Studies and Examples

Examining real-world examples and case studies of recording private businesses from public sidewalks can provide valuable insights into the challenges and successes of First Amendment audits. These case studies highlight effective strategies, lessons learned, and the impact of audits on businesses and communities. By understanding these examples, auditors can apply best practices to their own work and navigate similar situations more effectively.

Successful Audits

Successful audits often result in positive outcomes, such as increased transparency, improved accountability, and better public understanding of legal rights. Here are a few examples of successful audits of private businesses from public sidewalks:

1. **Retail Store Audit**: An auditor conducted an audit outside a popular retail store, documenting interactions with customers and employees. The auditor focused on public areas and avoided recording through windows or into private spaces. By clearly communicating the purpose of the audit and addressing any concerns respectfully, the auditor was able to conduct the audit without conflicts. The video gained significant attention online, raising awareness about the right to record in public spaces and promoting transparency in business operations.

2. **Restaurant Audit**: During an audit outside a busy restaurant, the auditor recorded interactions with patrons and staff. The auditor introduced themselves to the restaurant manager and explained the purpose of the audit. By maintaining a respectful and professional demeanor, the auditor built trust and conducted the audit smoothly. The video highlighted the importance of transparency in customer service and led to positive discussions about the role of audits in promoting accountability.
3. **Office Building Audit**: An auditor recorded outside an office building, documenting public interactions and activities. The auditor avoided recording through windows or into private offices, focusing instead on the exterior and public areas. By respecting privacy boundaries and communicating clearly with building staff, the auditor conducted the audit ethically and responsibly. The video demonstrated the auditor's commitment to transparency while respecting privacy, earning praise from viewers.

Lessons Learned

Analyzing key takeaways from notable case studies can provide valuable lessons for auditors. These lessons can help auditors refine their strategies and improve their effectiveness in future audits.

1. **Clear Communication**: Effective communication with business owners and employees is crucial for conducting successful audits. Introducing oneself, explaining the purpose of the audit, and addressing concerns respectfully can help build trust and reduce conflicts.
2. **Respecting Privacy**: Auditors must be mindful of privacy boundaries and avoid recording private conversations or sen-

sitive information. Focusing on public areas and interactions helps maintain ethical standards and respect for privacy.
3. **Professionalism and Respect**: Maintaining a respectful and professional demeanor is essential for building positive relationships with business owners, employees, and the public. This approach fosters trust and credibility, making it easier to conduct audits smoothly.
4. **Preparation and Research**: Thorough preparation and research are key to successful audits. Understanding the legal landscape, researching specific businesses, and being aware of potential challenges can help auditors navigate their work more effectively.

Impact on Businesses and Communities

Audits can have a significant impact on businesses and communities, leading to positive changes and improved transparency. Here are some examples of the impact of audits:

1. **Improved Transparency**: Audits can encourage businesses to operate more transparently, leading to better customer service and accountability. For example, a retail store that was audited may implement new policies to ensure that employees are well-informed about customers' rights and provide clear information to the public.
2. **Policy Changes**: Successful audits can prompt businesses to review and update their policies to align with legal standards and respect customers' rights. For instance, a restaurant that was audited may revise its policies to ensure that staff are trained on how to handle interactions with auditors and respect customers' rights to record in public areas.

3. **Community Awareness**: Audits can raise awareness about legal rights and the importance of transparency in business operations. By sharing their recordings and experiences, auditors can educate the public about their rights and encourage businesses to operate more openly and ethically.
4. **Positive Public Relations**: Businesses that respond positively to audits and demonstrate a commitment to transparency can benefit from positive public relations. Customers are more likely to trust and support businesses that operate openly and respect their rights.

Conclusion

Case studies and examples of recording private businesses from public sidewalks provide valuable insights into the challenges and successes of First Amendment audits. By examining successful audits, learning key lessons, and understanding the impact on businesses and communities, auditors can refine their strategies and conduct their work more effectively. Clear communication, respect for privacy, professionalism, and thorough preparation are essential for successful audits. Through their dedication to transparency and accountability, auditors contribute to a more open and just society, ensuring that public interactions and activities are documented responsibly and ethically.

Practical Tips for Auditors

Conducting audits of private businesses from public sidewalks requires careful preparation, effective communication, and a thorough understanding of legal and ethical considerations. This section provides practical tips for auditors, covering preparation and research, conducting the audit, handling confrontations, documenting and sharing audits, and building a support network. By following these guidelines, auditors can ensure their activities are effective, respectful, and legally sound.

Preparation and Research

Effective audits begin with thorough preparation and research. Understanding the legal landscape and specific businesses you plan to audit is crucial for a successful and conflict-free experience.

1. **Know the Laws**: Familiarize yourself with federal, state, and local laws regarding public recording. This includes understanding your rights under the First Amendment and any specific regulations that apply to recording from public sidewalks. Knowledge of relevant court cases, such as Glik v. Cunniffe and Turner v. Driver, can also be beneficial.
2. **Research the Business**: Before conducting an audit, research the specific business you plan to record. Understand its layout, public access areas, and any posted policies regarding recording. This information can help you navigate the area more effectively and avoid potential conflicts.
3. **Plan Your Approach**: Decide on the specific areas you want to audit and the interactions you aim to document. Having a clear plan can help you stay focused and organized during the audit.
4. **Prepare Your Equipment**: Ensure your recording equipment is in good working order. This includes checking your camera or smartphone, ensuring you have sufficient battery life and storage space, and having any necessary accessories, such as tripods or external microphones.

Conducting the Audit

When conducting the audit, it is essential to remain respectful, professional, and aware of your surroundings. The goal is to promote transparency and accountability without causing unnecessary disruptions.

1. **Introduce Yourself**: When you begin the audit, introduce yourself to any business owners or employees you encounter. Explain that you are conducting a First Amendment audit and briefly outline your rights to record from public sidewalks. This can help set a positive tone and reduce misunderstandings.
2. **Stay Calm and Respectful**: Maintain a calm and respectful demeanor throughout the audit. If you encounter resistance or hostility, respond politely and assertively, explaining your legal rights. Avoid escalating confrontations and remain focused on your objective.
3. **Focus on Public Areas**: Conduct your audit from public sidewalks, ensuring that you do not trespass onto private property. Avoid recording through windows or into private spaces where individuals have a reasonable expectation of privacy.
4. **Document Interactions**: Record your interactions with business owners, employees, and customers, focusing on how they respond to your presence and your right to record. Be mindful of capturing clear audio and video to ensure your documentation is effective.

Handling Confrontations and Challenges

Interactions with business owners and employees can sometimes be challenging. Understanding your rights and knowing how to handle these interactions is crucial.

1. **Know Your Rights**: Be well-versed in your legal rights to record from public sidewalks. This includes understanding the protections provided by the First Amendment and any relevant state laws. Familiarize yourself with key court rulings that support your right to record.
2. **Stay Composed**: If approached by business owners or employees, remain calm and composed. Clearly explain that you are conducting a First Amendment audit and outline your legal rights. Provide any relevant documentation or court rulings if necessary.
3. **Comply with Lawful Requests**: While you have the right to record from public sidewalks, it is essential to comply with lawful requests from business owners or employees. If asked to move to a different area or stop recording in a restricted space, comply respectfully while asserting your rights.
4. **Document the Interaction**: Record your interaction with business owners or employees, ensuring you capture clear audio and video. This documentation can be valuable if you need to address any legal challenges or complaints.

Documenting and Sharing Audits

Effective documentation and sharing of your audits are crucial for promoting transparency and accountability. Follow these tips to ensure your recordings are impactful and reach a broad audience.

1. **Review and Edit Footage**: After completing your audit, review your recordings to ensure they are clear and accurate. Edit the footage to remove any private conversations or sensitive information that may have been inadvertently captured.
2. **Provide Context**: When sharing your recordings, provide context for your audience. Explain the purpose of the audit,

the location, and any relevant legal information. This helps viewers understand the significance of your findings.
3. **Choose the Right Platforms**: Share your recordings on platforms that reach a broad audience and support your goals. Social media platforms like YouTube, Facebook, and Instagram are popular choices for auditors. Consider creating a dedicated channel or page for your audits to build a following and engage with your audience.
4. **Engage with Your Audience**: Encourage viewers to share your recordings and engage in discussions about the importance of transparency and accountability. Respond to comments and questions to foster a sense of community and support for your work.
5. **Maintain Professionalism**: When sharing your recordings, maintain a professional tone and focus on the facts. Avoid inflammatory language or personal attacks, as this can undermine the credibility of your work.

Building a Support Network

Building a support network is essential for conducting effective audits and promoting transparency and accountability. A strong network can provide resources, advice, and support when facing challenges.

1. **Community Support**: Engage with your local community and build relationships with individuals and organizations that support transparency and accountability. This can include civil liberties organizations, community groups, and other auditors.

2. **Collaboration**: Collaborate with other auditors and share your experiences and insights. Working together can help you learn from each other and improve your auditing practices.
3. **Legal Support**: Establish connections with legal professionals or organizations that can provide advice and representation if you face legal challenges. Having access to legal support can help you navigate complex situations and defend your rights.
4. **Public Awareness**: Raise public awareness about the importance of First Amendment audits and the right to record from public sidewalks. Educating the public can help build support for your work and promote a culture of transparency and accountability.

In conclusion, conducting audits of private businesses from public sidewalks requires careful preparation, effective communication, and a thorough understanding of legal and ethical considerations. By following these practical tips, auditors can ensure their activities are impactful, respectful, and legally sound. Through their dedication to transparency and accountability, auditors contribute to a more open and just society, ensuring that public interactions and activities are documented responsibly and ethically.

CHAPTER 7

Chapter 5: Practical Tips for First Amendment Audi

Preparation and Research
Effective First Amendment audits begin long before you step foot in a public space with your camera. Thorough preparation and research are essential to ensure that your audit is successful, respectful, and legally sound. This section provides detailed guidance on understanding your legal rights, researching locations, and planning your audit.

Understanding Legal Rights

Before conducting any audit, it is crucial to have a solid understanding of your legal rights under the First Amendment. This knowledge will empower you to assert your rights confidently and handle any challenges that may arise.

1. **Overview of First Amendment Protections**: The First Amendment guarantees freedoms concerning religion, expression, assembly, and the right to petition the government. For auditors, the most relevant protections are the freedoms

of speech and press, which include the right to record public officials and activities in public spaces.
2. **Key Legal Precedents and Landmark Cases**: Familiarize yourself with significant court cases that have defined and reinforced the right to record in public spaces. Notable cases include:
    - **Glik v. Cunniffe (2011)**: This case affirmed that the First Amendment protects the right to record public officials in public spaces.
    - **Turner v. Driver (2017)**: This ruling reinforced the right to record police officers from public sidewalks.
    - **Smith v. City of Cumming (2000)**: This decision upheld the right to record matters of public interest, including police activities.
3. **State-Specific Laws and Variations**: While the First Amendment provides broad protections, state laws can vary. Some states have enacted laws that explicitly protect the right to record public officials, while others may have more restrictive regulations. Research the specific laws in your state to ensure you are aware of any additional protections or limitations.

Researching Locations

Choosing the right locations for your audits is a critical step in the preparation process. Understanding the specific policies and regulations of each location will help you navigate potential challenges and conduct your audit smoothly.

1. **Identifying Public Buildings and Spaces for Audits**: Public buildings such as post offices, libraries, courthouses, and police stations are common targets for audits. These locations

are funded by taxpayer dollars and are generally open to the public, making them ideal for promoting transparency and accountability.
2. **Understanding Specific Policies and Regulations**: Each public building may have its own set of policies and regulations regarding public access and recording. Research these policies in advance to ensure you are aware of any restrictions or guidelines. For example, some courthouses may prohibit recording inside courtrooms, while libraries may have specific rules about recording during public meetings.
3. **Gathering Information on Past Incidents and Audits**: Reviewing past incidents and audits at your chosen locations can provide valuable insights into potential challenges and how to address them. Look for videos, articles, or reports from other auditors who have conducted audits at the same locations. This information can help you anticipate potential issues and develop strategies for handling them.

Planning the Audit

A well-planned audit is more likely to be successful and less likely to encounter significant challenges. Setting clear objectives, preparing necessary equipment, and developing a strategy for documenting interactions are all essential components of the planning process.

1. **Setting Clear Objectives and Goals**: Define what you hope to achieve with your audit. Are you aiming to test public officials' knowledge of First Amendment rights? Are you documenting public interactions to promote transparency? Having clear objectives will help you stay focused and measure the success of your audit.

2. **Preparing Necessary Equipment and Materials**: Ensure that your recording equipment is in good working order. This includes checking your camera or smartphone, ensuring you have sufficient battery life and storage space, and having any necessary accessories, such as tripods or external microphones. Additionally, consider carrying printed copies of relevant legal information or court rulings to provide to public officials if needed.
3. **Developing a Strategy for Documenting Interactions**: Plan how you will document your interactions during the audit. Decide which areas you will focus on, how you will approach public officials, and what specific interactions you aim to capture. Having a clear strategy will help you conduct your audit efficiently and effectively.

In conclusion, thorough preparation and research are essential for conducting successful First Amendment audits. By understanding your legal rights, researching locations, and planning your audit carefully, you can ensure that your activities are respectful, effective, and legally sound. This preparation will empower you to promote transparency and accountability while navigating potential challenges with confidence. Through diligent preparation, auditors can contribute to a more open and just society, ensuring that public interactions and activities are documented responsibly and ethically.

Conducting the Audit

Once you have thoroughly prepared and researched your audit, the next step is to conduct it effectively. This involves approaching public officials and employees with respect, recording interactions clearly and unobtrusively, and handling any confrontations or challenges that may arise. This section provides detailed guidance on these aspects to ensure your audit is successful and ethically conducted.

Approaching Public Officials and Employees

The way you approach public officials and employees can set the tone for your entire audit. A respectful and professional demeanor can help build trust and reduce resistance.

1. **Best Practices for Introducing Yourself and Explaining Your Purpose**: When you first arrive at the location, introduce yourself to any public officials or employees you encounter. Clearly explain that you are conducting a First Amendment audit and outline your rights to record in public spaces. Providing a brief explanation of your purpose can help alleviate concerns and foster cooperation.
2. **Strategies for Maintaining a Respectful and Professional Demeanor**: Throughout the audit, maintain a calm and respectful demeanor. Address public officials and employees politely, use appropriate language, and avoid confrontational behavior. Demonstrating professionalism can help build positive relationships and reduce the likelihood of conflicts.
3. **Handling Initial Resistance or Hostility**: If you encounter initial resistance or hostility, remain calm and composed. Politely assert your legal rights and provide any relevant documentation or information to support your position. Avoid escalating the situation and focus on maintaining a respectful dialogue.

Recording Interactions

Capturing clear and accurate recordings of your interactions is essential for documenting your audit. Effective recording techniques can help ensure that your footage is useful and impactful.

1. **Techniques for Capturing Clear Audio and Video**: Use high-quality recording equipment to capture clear audio and video. Ensure that your camera or smartphone is positioned to capture the interaction effectively, and use external microphones if necessary to improve audio quality. Pay attention to lighting and background noise to enhance the clarity of your recordings.
2. **Focusing on Public Areas and Avoiding Restricted Zones**: Conduct your audit in publicly accessible areas, such as lobbies, hallways, and public meeting rooms. Avoid restricted zones or areas where recording is prohibited. Respect any posted signs or instructions from public officials regarding restricted areas.
3. **Ensuring That Recordings Are Unobtrusive and Do Not Disrupt Operations**: While recording, be mindful of your surroundings and ensure that your activities do not disrupt the normal operations of the public building. Avoid blocking pathways, interfering with employees' work, or causing disturbances. Your goal is to document interactions without causing unnecessary disruptions.

Dealing with Confrontations

Confrontations can occur during audits, especially if public officials or employees are unaware of your legal rights. Knowing how to handle these situations effectively is crucial for maintaining the integrity of your audit.

1. **Staying Calm and Composed During Conflicts**: If a confrontation arises, remain calm and composed. Take deep breaths, speak slowly and clearly, and avoid raising your voice. Staying calm can help de-escalate the situation and demonstrate your professionalism.
2. **Legal Rights and Protections When Faced with Confrontations**: Be well-versed in your legal rights and protections under the First Amendment. If confronted, assert your right to record in public spaces and provide any relevant legal information or documentation. Familiarize yourself with key court rulings that support your position, such as Glik v. Cunniffe and Turner v. Driver.
3. **Steps to Take if Asked to Stop Recording or Leave the Premises**: If you are asked to stop recording or leave the premises, assess the situation carefully. If the request is lawful and reasonable, comply respectfully while asserting your rights. If you believe the request is unlawful or unjustified, calmly explain your legal rights and seek to resolve the situation through dialogue. If necessary, consider disengaging and seeking legal advice or support.

Case Studies of Effective Auditing

Examining case studies of effective auditing practices can provide valuable insights and lessons for auditors. These examples highlight how auditors can conduct their work responsibly and ethically.

1. **Library Audit**: An auditor conducted an audit in a public library, documenting interactions with staff and patrons. The auditor introduced themselves to the library staff and explained the purpose of the audit. By maintaining a respectful and professional demeanor, the auditor built trust and con-

ducted the audit without conflicts. The video highlighted the importance of transparency in public libraries and received positive feedback from viewers.
2. **Police Station Audit**: During an audit at a police station, the auditor recorded interactions with officers and documented public access areas. The auditor remained calm and composed when confronted by an officer who questioned their right to record. By providing relevant legal information and maintaining a respectful dialogue, the auditor was able to continue the audit and highlight the importance of transparency in law enforcement.
3. **Health Department Audit**: An auditor conducted an audit in the lobby of a health department, focusing on public interactions and avoiding areas where private health information was discussed. The auditor introduced themselves to the staff and explained the purpose of the audit. By respecting privacy boundaries and communicating clearly, the auditor conducted the audit ethically and effectively, raising awareness about the importance of transparency in public health services.

Conclusion

Conducting First Amendment audits requires a careful balance of respect, professionalism, and legal knowledge. By approaching public officials and employees with respect, capturing clear and unobtrusive recordings, and handling confrontations calmly and confidently, auditors can ensure their activities are effective and ethically conducted. Learning from case studies of effective auditing practices can provide valuable insights and help auditors refine their strategies. Through their dedication to transparency and accountability, auditors contribute to a more open and just society, ensuring that public interactions and activities are documented responsibly and ethically.

Documenting and Sharing Audits

Documenting and sharing your audits effectively is crucial for promoting transparency and accountability. High-quality recordings and thoughtful presentation can amplify the impact of your work, reaching a broad audience and fostering public awareness. This section provides detailed guidance on reviewing and editing footage, providing context, and sharing your audits on various platforms.

Reviewing and Editing Footage

After completing your audit, the first step is to review and edit your recordings. This process ensures that your footage is clear, accurate, and free of any private or sensitive information.

1. **Importance of Reviewing Recordings for Accuracy and Clarity**: Carefully review your recordings to ensure that they accurately capture the interactions and events you documented. Check for clear audio and video quality, and make sure that key moments are well-documented. Reviewing your footage helps you identify any issues that need to be addressed during the editing process.
2. **Editing Out Private Conversations or Sensitive Information**: During your review, look for any private conversations or sensitive information that may have been inadvertently captured. Edit out these sections to respect individuals' privacy and maintain ethical standards. This step is crucial for ensuring that your final footage is respectful and legally compliant.
3. **Ensuring That the Final Footage Is Concise and Impactful**: Aim to create a final video that is concise and impact-

ful. Trim any unnecessary or repetitive sections to keep the viewer's attention focused on the key interactions and findings. A well-edited video is more likely to engage viewers and effectively convey your message.

Providing Context

Providing context for your recordings is essential for helping viewers understand the significance of your audit. Clear explanations and relevant background information can enhance the impact of your footage.

1. **Explaining the Purpose and Significance of the Audit**: When sharing your recordings, include a clear explanation of the purpose and significance of your audit. Describe why you chose the specific location, what you aimed to achieve, and how the audit contributes to promoting transparency and accountability. This context helps viewers appreciate the importance of your work.
2. **Including Relevant Legal Information and Background Details**: Provide relevant legal information and background details to support your audit. This can include references to key legal precedents, explanations of your rights under the First Amendment, and any specific regulations or policies related to the location. Including this information helps viewers understand the legal framework that supports your audit.
3. **Highlighting Key Interactions and Findings**: Emphasize the key interactions and findings from your audit. Highlight moments that demonstrate public officials' knowledge (or lack thereof) of First Amendment rights, instances of respectful and professional behavior, and any challenges or conflicts

you encountered. Focusing on these highlights makes your video more engaging and informative.

Sharing on Platforms

Choosing the right platforms and engaging with your audience effectively can maximize the reach and impact of your audits. Consider the following tips for sharing your recordings:

1. **Choosing the Right Platforms for Maximum Reach and Impact**: Select platforms that will help you reach a broad audience and achieve your goals. Social media platforms like YouTube, Facebook, and Instagram are popular choices for auditors. Each platform has its own strengths, so consider where your target audience is most active and engaged.
2. **Engaging with Viewers and Responding to Comments**: Actively engage with viewers by responding to comments and questions. Encourage discussions about the importance of transparency and accountability, and be open to feedback. Engaging with your audience helps build a sense of community and support for your work.
3. **Building a Following and Fostering Community Support**: Consistently share high-quality content and engage with your audience to build a following. Consider creating a dedicated channel or page for your audits, where viewers can find all your recordings and updates. Fostering a supportive community can amplify the impact of your work and encourage others to get involved in promoting transparency.

Case Studies of Effective Documentation and Sharing

Examining case studies of effective documentation and sharing practices can provide valuable insights and lessons for auditors.

These examples highlight how auditors can maximize the impact of their work through thoughtful presentation and engagement.

1. **Library Audit**: An auditor conducted an audit in a public library, documenting interactions with staff and patrons. The auditor reviewed and edited the footage to remove any private conversations and provided a clear explanation of the audit's purpose. The video was shared on YouTube, where it received positive feedback and sparked discussions about the importance of transparency in public libraries.
2. **Police Station Audit**: During an audit at a police station, the auditor recorded interactions with officers and documented public access areas. The auditor provided context by including references to relevant legal precedents and explaining the significance of the audit. The video was shared on Facebook, where it reached a broad audience and raised awareness about the right to record police officers.
3. **Health Department Audit**: An auditor conducted an audit in the lobby of a health department, focusing on public interactions and avoiding areas where private health information was discussed. The auditor reviewed and edited the footage to ensure it was respectful and legally compliant. The video was shared on Instagram, where it received positive feedback and highlighted the importance of transparency in public health services.

Conclusion

Documenting and sharing your audits effectively is crucial for promoting transparency and accountability. By reviewing and editing footage carefully, providing clear context, and engaging with your audience on the right platforms, you can maximize the impact of your work. Learning from case studies of effective documentation and sharing practices can provide valuable insights and help you refine your strategies. Through thoughtful presentation and active engagement, auditors can contribute to a more open and just society, ensuring that public interactions and activities are documented responsibly and ethically.

Building a Support Network

Building a robust support network is essential for First Amendment auditors. A strong network can provide resources, advice, and support, helping auditors navigate challenges and amplify their impact. This section explores the importance of community support, strategies for collaborating with other auditors, and seeking legal and professional support.

Engaging with the Community

Community support is a cornerstone of successful First Amendment audits. Engaging with your local community can help build relationships, foster understanding, and create a supportive environment for your work.

1. **Importance of Community Support for Successful Audits**: Community support can provide a foundation of trust and cooperation, making it easier to conduct audits and address challenges. When the community understands and supports your goals, they are more likely to engage positively with your work and advocate for transparency and accountability.
2. **Strategies for Building Relationships with Local Organizations and Groups**: Identify and connect with local organizations and groups that share your commitment to transparency and accountability. This can include civil liberties organizations, community advocacy groups, and local media outlets. Attend community meetings, participate in

events, and engage in discussions to build relationships and foster collaboration.
3. **Participating in Community Events and Discussions**: Actively participate in community events and discussions to raise awareness about your work and the importance of First Amendment audits. This can include speaking at public forums, hosting informational sessions, and engaging with community members on social media. By being visible and approachable, you can build a network of supporters and allies.

Collaborating with Other Auditors

Collaboration with other auditors can enhance your effectiveness and provide valuable insights and resources. Working together can help you learn from each other's experiences and coordinate efforts for greater impact.

1. **Benefits of Working with Other Auditors**: Collaborating with other auditors can provide mutual support, share knowledge and resources, and amplify your collective impact. By working together, you can address challenges more effectively and achieve common goals.
2. **Sharing Experiences, Tips, and Resources**: Regularly communicate with other auditors to share experiences, tips, and resources. This can include discussing successful strategies, sharing legal information, and providing feedback on each other's work. Online forums, social media groups, and in-person meetings can facilitate these exchanges.
3. **Coordinating Joint Audits and Projects**: Consider coordinating joint audits and projects with other auditors. Joint audits can provide additional support and resources, making

it easier to conduct comprehensive audits and address challenges. Collaborative projects, such as creating educational materials or hosting community events, can also amplify your impact and reach a broader audience.

Seeking Legal and Professional Support

Having access to legal and professional support is crucial for navigating complex situations and defending your rights. Building a network of advisors and advocates can provide valuable guidance and resources.

1. **Identifying Legal Professionals and Organizations That Support First Amendment Rights**: Research and connect with legal professionals and organizations that specialize in First Amendment rights and civil liberties. This can include attorneys, legal advocacy groups, and nonprofit organizations. Establishing these connections can provide you with expert advice and representation if needed.
2. **Building a Network of Advisors and Advocates**: Develop relationships with advisors and advocates who can provide guidance and support. This can include legal professionals, experienced auditors, and community leaders. Regularly communicate with your network to seek advice, share updates, and discuss challenges.
3. **Accessing Resources and Training for Legal Challenges**: Take advantage of resources and training opportunities to enhance your knowledge and skills. This can include attending workshops, participating in webinars, and accessing online resources. Staying informed about legal developments and best practices can help you navigate challenges more effectively and defend your rights.

Case Studies of Building a Support Network

Examining case studies of auditors who have successfully built support networks can provide valuable insights and lessons. These examples highlight the importance of community engagement, collaboration, and legal support.

1. **Community Engagement**: An auditor built strong community support by regularly attending local government meetings and engaging with community members on social media. By being visible and approachable, the auditor fostered a sense of trust and cooperation, making it easier to conduct audits and address challenges.
2. **Collaboration with Other Auditors**: A group of auditors formed a collaborative network to share resources, coordinate joint audits, and provide mutual support. By working together, they were able to conduct more comprehensive audits and amplify their impact. The network also provided a platform for sharing experiences and learning from each other's successes and challenges.
3. **Legal and Professional Support**: An auditor faced legal challenges after conducting an audit at a public building. By connecting with a legal advocacy organization, the auditor received expert advice and representation, successfully defending their rights. The support network provided valuable resources and guidance, helping the auditor navigate the legal process and continue their work.

Conclusion

Building a support network is essential for First Amendment auditors. Engaging with the community, collaborating with other auditors, and seeking legal and professional support can provide valuable resources, advice, and support. By fostering relationships, sharing knowledge, and accessing expert guidance, auditors can navigate challenges more effectively and amplify their impact. Through their dedication to transparency and accountability, auditors contribute to a more open and just society, ensuring that public interactions and activities are documented responsibly and ethically.

Promoting Positive Change

First Amendment audits are not just about documenting interactions and holding public officials accountable; they are also about promoting positive change in society. By highlighting success stories, advocating for policy changes, and educating the public, auditors can make a significant impact. This section explores how auditors can use their findings to promote positive change, share success stories, advocate for reforms, and educate the public.

Highlighting Success Stories

Sharing examples of successful audits that have led to positive outcomes can inspire others and demonstrate the impact of transparency and accountability.

1. **Sharing Examples of Audits That Led to Positive Outcomes**: Highlight audits that have resulted in tangible improvements, such as policy changes, increased transparency, or enhanced public trust. For example, an audit at a police station that led to the implementation of body-worn cameras can serve as a powerful example of how audits can drive positive change.
2. **Testimonials from Auditors and Community Members**: Include testimonials from auditors and community members who have witnessed the positive impact of audits. Personal stories and experiences can add a human element to your findings and make them more relatable and compelling.

3. **Demonstrating the Impact of Transparency and Accountability**: Use your findings to show how transparency and accountability benefit society. Highlight specific examples of how audits have improved public services, increased trust in government institutions, and empowered citizens to exercise their rights.

Advocating for Policy Changes

Using your audit findings to advocate for policy changes and reforms can lead to long-term improvements in transparency and accountability.

1. **Using Audit Findings to Advocate for Reforms and Improvements**: Present your audit findings to policymakers, public officials, and community leaders to advocate for specific reforms. For example, if your audit reveals a lack of transparency in a public institution, use your findings to push for the implementation of transparency measures, such as public access to records or regular audits.
2. **Engaging with Policymakers and Public Officials**: Build relationships with policymakers and public officials to advocate for changes. Attend public meetings, participate in consultations, and engage in discussions to present your findings and recommendations. Effective advocacy requires clear communication and a collaborative approach.
3. **Participating in Public Hearings and Consultations**: Take advantage of opportunities to participate in public hearings and consultations. Present your audit findings and recommendations to decision-makers, and use these platforms to raise awareness about the importance of transparency and accountability.

Educating the Public

Raising public awareness about First Amendment rights and the importance of audits is crucial for fostering a culture of transparency and accountability.

1. **Raising Awareness About First Amendment Rights and the Importance of Audits**: Create educational content that explains First Amendment rights and the role of audits in promoting transparency. Use videos, articles, social media posts, and public presentations to reach a broad audience and raise awareness.
2. **Creating Educational Content and Resources**: Develop resources such as guides, infographics, and videos that explain the legal rights to record in public spaces, the importance of transparency, and best practices for conducting audits. Make these resources accessible to the public through your website, social media, and community events.
3. **Encouraging Others to Become Involved in Promoting Transparency and Accountability**: Inspire others to get involved in promoting transparency and accountability. Share success stories, provide guidance on how to conduct audits, and encourage community members to participate in public meetings and advocate for their rights. Building a network of engaged citizens can amplify your impact and drive positive change.

Case Studies of Promoting Positive Change

Examining case studies of auditors who have successfully promoted positive change can provide valuable insights and lessons. These examples highlight how auditors can use their findings to drive reforms and educate the public.

1. **Police Station Audit Leading to Policy Changes**: An auditor conducted an audit at a police station, documenting interactions with officers and highlighting a lack of transparency. The findings were presented to local policymakers, leading to the implementation of body-worn cameras and improved training for officers. The audit demonstrated the power of transparency in driving policy changes and improving public trust.
2. **Library Audit Raising Public Awareness**: During an audit at a public library, the auditor documented interactions with staff and patrons and highlighted the importance of transparency in public institutions. The findings were shared through social media and community presentations, raising awareness about First Amendment rights and the role of audits. The audit inspired community members to advocate for greater transparency in other public institutions.
3. **Health Department Audit Leading to Reforms**: An auditor conducted an audit in the lobby of a health department, focusing on public interactions and avoiding areas where private health information was discussed. The findings revealed a need for greater transparency in public health services. The auditor presented the findings to health department officials, leading to the implementation of new transparency measures and improved public access to information.

Conclusion

Promoting positive change is a key goal of First Amendment audits. By highlighting success stories, advocating for policy changes, and educating the public, auditors can make a significant impact on transparency and accountability. Sharing examples of successful audits, engaging with policymakers, and creating educational content are essential strategies for driving reforms and raising awareness. Through their dedication to promoting positive change, auditors contribute to a more open and just society, ensuring that public institutions operate transparently and ethically. By inspiring others to get involved and advocating for reforms, auditors help build a culture of transparency and accountability that benefits everyone.

CHAPTER 8

Chapter 6: Positive Impacts of First Amendment Aud

Enhancing Government Transparency

First Amendment audits play a crucial role in enhancing government transparency, a fundamental principle of democratic governance. By promoting open access to information, improving public trust, and encouraging open government practices, these audits help ensure that public institutions operate with integrity and accountability. This section explores how First Amendment audits contribute to increased transparency and provides examples of their positive impact.

Increased Public Access to Information

One of the primary goals of First Amendment audits is to promote open access to government records and activities. Auditors document their interactions with public officials and share their findings with the public, shedding light on the inner workings of government institutions. This transparency is essential for holding public officials accountable and ensuring that government actions are conducted in the public interest.

1. **How Audits Promote Open Access to Government Records and Activities**: Auditors often request access to public records, attend public meetings, and document their interactions with government officials. By doing so, they help ensure that government activities are open to public scrutiny. This transparency allows citizens to stay informed about government decisions and actions, fostering a more engaged and informed public.
2. **Examples of Audits Leading to the Release of Previously Withheld Information**: There have been numerous instances where audits have led to the release of information that was previously withheld from the public. For example, an audit at a city hall might reveal discrepancies in budget allocations, prompting the release of detailed financial records. Similarly, an audit at a police department might uncover instances of misconduct, leading to the release of internal investigation reports. These examples demonstrate how audits can uncover important information and promote greater transparency.

Improving Public Trust

Transparency is a key factor in building and maintaining public trust in government institutions. When government actions are open to scrutiny, citizens are more likely to trust that officials are acting in their best interests. First Amendment audits help restore and enhance this trust by providing a clear and accurate account of government activities.

1. **The Role of Transparency in Building Trust Between the Public and Government**: Trust in government is built on the foundation of transparency and accountability. When citizens have access to information about government actions

and decisions, they can hold officials accountable and ensure that their interests are represented. Audits play a vital role in this process by documenting and sharing information that might otherwise remain hidden.

2. **Case Studies of Audits That Have Restored Public Confidence in Institutions**: There are numerous case studies that highlight the positive impact of audits on public trust. For example, an audit of a local school board might reveal issues with transparency in decision-making processes. By documenting these issues and advocating for greater openness, auditors can help restore public confidence in the school board. Similarly, an audit of a municipal government might uncover instances of corruption, leading to reforms that enhance transparency and accountability. These case studies demonstrate how audits can rebuild trust in public institutions.

Encouraging Open Government Practices

First Amendment audits incentivize government agencies to adopt more transparent practices. When public officials know that their actions are being documented and scrutinized, they are more likely to operate openly and ethically. This shift towards transparency can lead to significant improvements in government practices and policies.

1. **How Audits Incentivize Government Agencies to Adopt More Transparent Practices**: The presence of auditors acts as a deterrent to unethical behavior and encourages public officials to adhere to best practices for transparency. Knowing that their actions are subject to public scrutiny, officials are

more likely to follow proper procedures, provide accurate information, and engage with the public openly.
2. **Examples of Policy Changes and Reforms Prompted by Audits**: Audits have led to numerous policy changes and reforms aimed at enhancing transparency. For example, an audit of a public health department might reveal a lack of transparency in reporting health data. In response, the department might implement new policies to ensure that health information is readily accessible to the public. Similarly, an audit of a city council might uncover issues with transparency in decision-making processes, leading to the adoption of new procedures for public meetings and record-keeping. These examples highlight how audits can drive meaningful reforms that promote open government practices.

Conclusion

First Amendment audits are a powerful tool for enhancing government transparency. By promoting open access to information, improving public trust, and encouraging open government practices, audits help ensure that public institutions operate with integrity and accountability. The positive impact of audits is evident in the increased transparency, restored public confidence, and policy reforms they inspire. Through their dedication to transparency and accountability, auditors contribute to a more open and just society, ensuring that government actions are conducted in the public interest and subject to public scrutiny.

Holding Public Officials Accountable

First Amendment audits are instrumental in holding public officials accountable for their actions. By documenting misconduct, promoting ethical behavior, and strengthening oversight mechanisms, these audits ensure that public officials adhere to the highest standards of conduct. This section explores how First Amendment audits contribute to accountability and provides examples of their positive impact.

Documenting Misconduct and Abuse

One of the most significant contributions of First Amendment audits is their ability to document instances of misconduct and abuse by public officials. By recording interactions and sharing their findings, auditors provide concrete evidence that can lead to disciplinary actions, legal proceedings, and systemic reforms.

1. **The Importance of Recording and Exposing Instances of Misconduct**: Recording interactions with public officials serves as a powerful tool for exposing misconduct and abuse. Auditors capture real-time evidence of inappropriate behavior, violations of rights, and unethical practices. This documentation is crucial for holding officials accountable and ensuring that they face consequences for their actions.
2. **Notable Cases Where Audits Have Led to Disciplinary Actions or Legal Proceedings**: There are numerous examples of audits leading to significant consequences for public officials. For instance, an audit at a police department might reveal instances of excessive force or discriminatory practices. The recorded evidence can prompt internal investigations, resulting in disciplinary actions against the officers involved. In some cases, the evidence gathered by auditors has led to criminal charges and legal proceedings, ensuring that justice is served.

Promoting Ethical Behavior

The presence of auditors can have a deterrent effect on unethical behavior by public officials. Knowing that their actions are being recorded and scrutinized, officials are more likely to adhere to ethical standards and conduct themselves appropriately.

1. **How the Presence of Auditors Can Deter Unethical Behavior by Public Officials**: The knowledge that auditors are documenting their actions can encourage public officials to act ethically and responsibly. This deterrent effect helps prevent misconduct and promotes a culture of accountability within public institutions. Officials are more likely to follow proper procedures, treat citizens with respect, and avoid actions that could be perceived as unethical.
2. **Examples of Improved Conduct and Accountability Resulting from Audits**: Audits have led to noticeable improvements in the conduct of public officials. For example, an audit at a city council meeting might reveal instances of officials disregarding public input or making decisions behind closed doors. The exposure of these practices can lead to changes in how meetings are conducted, ensuring greater transparency and public participation. Similarly, an audit at a public health department might highlight issues with how services are delivered, prompting reforms that improve accountability and service quality.

Strengthening Oversight Mechanisms

First Amendment audits play a crucial role in strengthening both internal and external oversight mechanisms within public institutions. By highlighting areas where oversight is lacking, audits can prompt the establishment of new procedures and bodies to ensure greater accountability.

1. **The Role of Audits in Enhancing Internal and External Oversight of Public Institutions**: Audits can reveal gaps in existing oversight mechanisms, prompting institutions to implement new procedures to monitor and evaluate the actions of public officials. This enhanced oversight helps ensure that officials are held accountable for their actions and that any issues are addressed promptly and effectively.
2. **Case Studies of Audits Leading to the Establishment of New Oversight Bodies or Procedures**: There are several examples of audits leading to the creation of new oversight bodies or the implementation of improved procedures. For instance, an audit of a municipal government might uncover issues with financial management and transparency. In response, the government might establish an independent oversight committee to review financial practices and ensure compliance with ethical standards. Similarly, an audit of a police department might reveal deficiencies in how complaints are handled, leading to the creation of a civilian review board to oversee investigations and ensure accountability.

Conclusion

First Amendment audits are a powerful tool for holding public officials accountable. By documenting misconduct, promoting ethical behavior, and strengthening oversight mechanisms, audits ensure that public officials adhere to the highest standards of conduct. The positive impact of audits is evident in the disciplinary actions, legal proceedings, and systemic reforms they inspire. Through their dedication to accountability and transparency, auditors contribute to a more just and ethical society, ensuring that public officials are held responsible for their actions and that public institutions operate with integrity. By promoting a culture of accountability, auditors help build trust between the public and government, fostering a more engaged and informed citizenry.

Empowering Citizens and Communities

First Amendment audits do more than just hold public officials accountable; they also play a crucial role in empowering citizens and communities. By educating the public about their rights, fostering civic engagement, and building community solidarity, these audits help create a more informed and active citizenry. This section explores how First Amendment audits empower individuals and communities and provides examples of their positive impact.

Educating the Public About Their Rights

One of the most significant benefits of First Amendment audits is their ability to educate the public about their constitutional rights. Many citizens are unaware of their rights under the First Amendment, and audits serve as a powerful tool for raising awareness and promoting understanding.

1. **How Audits Raise Awareness of First Amendment Rights and Civil Liberties**: Auditors often engage with the public during their audits, explaining the legal basis for their activities and the importance of transparency and accountability. By documenting their interactions and sharing their findings, auditors help educate the public about their rights to free speech, press, and assembly. This increased awareness empowers individuals to exercise their rights and advocate for themselves and their communities.

2. **Examples of Educational Initiatives and Resources Developed by Auditors**: Many auditors go beyond their fieldwork to create educational resources that further promote understanding of First Amendment rights. For example, an auditor might develop informational videos, write articles, or

create guides that explain the legal framework for public recording and the importance of transparency. These resources can be shared through social media, community events, and educational workshops, reaching a broad audience and fostering a more informed public.

Fostering Civic Engagement

First Amendment audits encourage citizens to become more actively involved in their communities and government processes. By highlighting issues of public concern and demonstrating the impact of civic participation, audits inspire individuals to engage in meaningful ways.

1. **The Impact of Audits on Encouraging Public Participation in Government Processes**: Audits often reveal areas where public institutions can improve, prompting citizens to take action. For example, an audit might uncover a lack of transparency in a local government agency, leading community members to attend public meetings, submit public records requests, or advocate for policy changes. This increased participation helps ensure that government actions reflect the needs and interests of the community.
2. **Stories of Communities Mobilizing for Change as a Result of Audit Findings**: There are numerous examples of communities mobilizing for change in response to audit findings. For instance, an audit of a school board might reveal issues with how decisions are made, prompting parents and community members to organize and advocate for greater transparency and accountability. Similarly, an audit of a police department might highlight concerns about policing practices, leading to community-led efforts to reform law enforce-

ment policies. These stories demonstrate the power of audits to inspire collective action and drive positive change.

Building Community Solidarity

First Amendment audits can unite communities around common goals of transparency and accountability. By working together to address issues of public concern, community members can build stronger, more cohesive communities.

1. **How Audits Can Unite Communities Around Common Goals of Transparency and Accountability**: Audits often bring to light issues that affect the entire community, creating a shared sense of purpose and urgency. Community members can come together to support auditors, advocate for reforms, and hold public officials accountable. This collective effort helps build a sense of solidarity and strengthens the community's ability to effect change.
2. **Examples of Community-Led Initiatives Inspired by Audit Activities**: Audits have inspired numerous community-led initiatives aimed at promoting transparency and accountability. For example, a community might establish a citizen oversight committee to monitor local government activities, or organize public forums to discuss audit findings and develop action plans. These initiatives not only address specific issues but also foster a culture of civic engagement and collective responsibility.

Conclusion

First Amendment audits play a vital role in empowering citizens and communities. By educating the public about their rights, fostering civic engagement, and building community solidarity, audits help create a more informed and active citizenry. The positive impact of audits is evident in the increased awareness, participation, and collective action they inspire. Through their dedication to transparency and accountability, auditors contribute to a more open and just society, ensuring that citizens are empowered to exercise their rights and advocate for their communities. By promoting a culture of civic engagement and collective responsibility, auditors help build stronger, more resilient communities that are better equipped to address challenges and drive positive change.

Driving Policy and Legislative Reforms

First Amendment audits have the power to drive significant policy and legislative reforms. By using audit findings to influence policy changes, advocating for broader legislative reforms, and enhancing legal protections for auditors, these activities contribute to systemic improvements that promote transparency and accountability. This section explores how First Amendment audits can drive policy and legislative reforms and provides examples of their positive impact.

Influencing Policy Changes

Audit findings can serve as a catalyst for policy changes within public institutions. By highlighting areas where improvements are needed, auditors can inform and shape public policy, leading to more transparent and accountable governance.

1. **How Audit Findings Can Inform and Shape Public Policy**: Auditors document their interactions with public officials and identify areas where policies and practices fall short. These findings can be presented to policymakers, public officials, and community leaders to advocate for specific reforms. For example, an audit might reveal a lack of transparency in how a city council conducts its meetings. The findings can

prompt the council to adopt new policies that ensure meetings are open to the public and that records are readily accessible.

2. **Examples of Specific Policy Changes Driven by Audit Results**: There are numerous examples of audits leading to meaningful policy changes. For instance, an audit of a police department might uncover issues with how complaints against officers are handled. The findings could lead to the implementation of new procedures for investigating complaints and ensuring accountability. Similarly, an audit of a public health department might reveal deficiencies in how health data is reported, prompting the department to adopt new policies for data transparency and public reporting.

Advocating for Legislative Reforms

Beyond influencing specific policies, First Amendment audits can also drive broader legislative reforms that protect civil liberties and promote transparency.

1. **The Role of Auditors in Pushing for Broader Legislative Changes to Protect Civil Liberties**: Auditors can use their findings to advocate for legislative changes that strengthen protections for civil liberties. This can include lobbying for new laws or amendments that safeguard the right to record in public spaces, protect whistleblowers, and ensure government transparency. By engaging with legislators and participating in the legislative process, auditors can help shape laws that promote accountability and protect individual rights.

2. **Case Studies of Successful Legislative Advocacy Efforts by Auditors**: There are several examples of auditors successfully advocating for legislative reforms. For instance, an audit

might reveal that existing laws do not adequately protect the right to record public officials. In response, auditors could work with legislators to draft and pass new legislation that explicitly protects this right. Another example might involve advocating for laws that require public institutions to adopt transparency measures, such as regular audits and public access to records. These legislative efforts help create a legal framework that supports transparency and accountability.

Enhancing Legal Protections for Auditors

First Amendment audits have also contributed to strengthening legal protections for those who record in public spaces. By highlighting the challenges and risks faced by auditors, these activities can inspire new laws or amendments that provide greater legal safeguards.

1. **How Audits Have Contributed to Strengthening Legal Protections for Those Who Record in Public Spaces**: Auditors often face legal challenges, such as harassment, arrests, or lawsuits, for exercising their right to record. By documenting these challenges and advocating for legal reforms, auditors can help strengthen protections for themselves and others. This can include pushing for laws that prohibit retaliation against auditors, protect their right to record, and ensure that any legal actions taken against them are subject to strict scrutiny.
2. **Examples of New Laws or Amendments Inspired by Audit Activities**: There are several instances where audit activities have inspired new laws or amendments. For example, an audit might reveal that auditors are frequently harassed or arrested for recording public officials. In response, legislators could pass laws that explicitly protect auditors from such ac-

tions and provide legal remedies for those who face retaliation. Another example might involve amending existing laws to clarify and strengthen the right to record in public spaces, ensuring that auditors can conduct their work without fear of legal repercussions.

Conclusion

First Amendment audits play a crucial role in driving policy and legislative reforms. By using audit findings to influence policy changes, advocating for broader legislative reforms, and enhancing legal protections for auditors, these activities contribute to systemic improvements that promote transparency and accountability. The positive impact of audits is evident in the policy changes, legislative reforms, and strengthened legal protections they inspire. Through their dedication to promoting positive change, auditors contribute to a more open and just society, ensuring that public institutions operate transparently and ethically. By advocating for reforms and engaging in the legislative process, auditors help create a legal framework that supports transparency and accountability, benefiting everyone.

Inspiring a Culture of Accountability

First Amendment audits have the potential to inspire a broader culture of accountability within public institutions and communities. By creating a ripple effect, encouraging responsible auditing practices, and sustaining long-term impact, these audits contribute to systemic changes that promote transparency and ethical behavior. This section explores how First Amendment audits inspire a culture of accountability and provides examples of their positive impact.

Creating a Ripple Effect

Individual audits can have a far-reaching impact, inspiring others to take up the cause of transparency and accountability. The actions of one auditor can set off a chain reaction, leading to broader movements and systemic changes.

1. **How Individual Audits Can Inspire Broader Movements for Transparency and Accountability**: When auditors document and share their findings, they raise awareness about issues of public concern and demonstrate the power of civic engagement. This visibility can inspire others to conduct their own audits, advocate for reforms, and hold public officials accountable. The ripple effect of individual audits can lead to a collective effort to promote transparency and accountability across various institutions and communities.
2. **Stories of Auditors Who Have Inspired Others to Take Up the Cause**: There are numerous examples of auditors who have inspired others to join the movement for transparency and accountability. For instance, an auditor who exposes corruption in a local government might inspire community members to conduct their own audits and advocate for reforms. Similarly, an auditor who documents police misconduct might motivate others to monitor law enforcement practices and push for greater accountability. These stories highlight the transformative power of individual actions and their ability to inspire broader change.

Encouraging Responsible Auditing Practices

Maintaining public support for First Amendment audits requires auditors to conduct their work ethically and responsibly. By adhering to best practices and guidelines, auditors can ensure that their activities are respected and valued by the community.

1. **The Importance of Ethical and Respectful Auditing Practices in Maintaining Public Support**: Ethical and respectful auditing practices are essential for building and maintaining public trust. Auditors must balance their right to record with respect for privacy and the need to avoid unnecessary disruptions. By conducting audits responsibly, auditors can demonstrate their commitment to transparency and accountability while maintaining public support.
2. **Examples of Best Practices and Guidelines Developed by the Auditing Community**: The auditing community has developed various best practices and guidelines to ensure that audits are conducted ethically and effectively. These guidelines include respecting privacy boundaries, avoiding confrontational behavior, and focusing on public areas and interactions. By following these best practices, auditors can conduct their work in a manner that is both impactful and respectful.

Sustaining Long-Term Impact

Ensuring the lasting impact of audit activities requires a strategic approach that focuses on long-term goals and systemic changes. Auditors must work to sustain the momentum generated by their audits and continue to advocate for transparency and accountability.

1. **Strategies for Ensuring the Lasting Impact of Audit Activities**: To sustain the impact of their work, auditors should focus on building strong support networks, engaging with policymakers, and advocating for systemic reforms. This includes collaborating with other auditors, community organizations, and legal professionals to address challenges and drive long-term change. Additionally, auditors should con-

tinue to document and share their findings, raising awareness and keeping the public informed.
2. **Case Studies of Audits That Have Led to Sustained Improvements in Government Transparency and Accountability**: There are several examples of audits that have led to sustained improvements in government transparency and accountability. For instance, an audit of a city council might result in the implementation of new transparency measures, such as regular public meetings and accessible records. These changes can have a lasting impact, ensuring that the council operates openly and ethically. Similarly, an audit of a police department might lead to the establishment of a civilian oversight board, providing ongoing accountability and oversight. These case studies demonstrate how audits can drive long-term improvements and create a culture of accountability.

Conclusion

First Amendment audits have the power to inspire a culture of accountability within public institutions and communities. By creating a ripple effect, encouraging responsible auditing practices, and sustaining long-term impact, these audits contribute to systemic changes that promote transparency and ethical behavior. The positive impact of audits is evident in the broader movements, ethical practices, and sustained improvements they inspire. Through their dedication to transparency and accountability, auditors contribute to a more open and just society, ensuring that public institutions operate with integrity and that citizens are empowered to hold their government accountable. By fostering a culture of accountability, auditors help build a foundation for lasting change and a more engaged and informed citizenry.

CHAPTER 9

Conclusion

Recap of Key Themes and Findings

As we reach the conclusion of this book, it is essential to reflect on the key themes and findings that have emerged from our exploration of First Amendment audits. These audits play a critical role in promoting transparency, accountability, and public trust in government institutions. By documenting interactions with public officials and sharing their findings, auditors help ensure that government actions are conducted openly and ethically. This section recaps the importance of First Amendment audits, revisits the role of auditors, and highlights the impact of audits on public awareness and engagement.

Summary of the Importance of First Amendment Audits

First Amendment audits are a powerful tool for promoting transparency and accountability within public institutions. Throughout this book, we have seen how audits can uncover instances of misconduct, drive policy changes, and restore public trust. By exercising their constitutional rights to record in public spaces, auditors provide a check on government power and ensure that officials are held accountable for their actions.

1. **Overview of How Audits Promote Transparency, Accountability, and Public Trust**: Audits promote transparency by documenting government activities and making this information accessible to the public. This openness allows citizens to stay informed about government decisions and actions, fostering a more engaged and informed public. Accountability is achieved by exposing instances of misconduct and unethical behavior, prompting disciplinary actions and reforms. Public trust is restored when citizens see that government institutions are operating transparently and ethically.
2. **Key Findings from the Book That Highlight the Impact of Audits on Public Institutions**: Throughout the chapters, we have explored numerous examples of how audits have led to positive changes in public institutions. From policy reforms and legislative changes to increased public awareness and civic engagement, the impact of audits is far-reaching. These findings underscore the importance of continued efforts to promote transparency and accountability through First Amendment audits.

Revisiting the Role of Auditors

Auditors play an essential role in safeguarding civil liberties and promoting open government. Their dedication to transparency and accountability helps ensure that public institutions operate with integrity and respect for citizens' rights.

1. **The Essential Role Auditors Play in Safeguarding Civil Liberties and Promoting Open Government**: Auditors act as watchdogs, monitoring government activities and documenting interactions with public officials. By exercising their

First Amendment rights, they help protect civil liberties and promote a culture of transparency and accountability. Auditors' work is crucial for maintaining a healthy democracy where government actions are subject to public scrutiny.

2. **Examples of Auditors Who Have Made Significant Contributions to Transparency and Accountability**: Throughout this book, we have highlighted several auditors who have made significant contributions to promoting transparency and accountability. These individuals have exposed instances of misconduct, driven policy changes, and inspired others to join the movement for open government. Their dedication and perseverance serve as an inspiration to all who seek to hold public officials accountable.

Impact on Public Awareness and Engagement

First Amendment audits have a profound impact on public awareness and engagement. By raising awareness about constitutional rights and encouraging civic participation, audits empower citizens to take an active role in their communities and government processes.

1. **How Audits Have Raised Public Awareness About First Amendment Rights and Encouraged Civic Participation**: Auditors often engage with the public during their audits, explaining the legal basis for their activities and the importance of transparency and accountability. By documenting and sharing their findings, auditors help educate the public about their rights and the role of audits in promoting open government. This increased awareness empowers individuals to exercise their rights and advocate for themselves and their communities.

2. **Stories of Communities That Have Been Empowered by Audit Activities**: There are numerous stories of communities that have been empowered by audit activities. For example, an audit might reveal issues with transparency in a local government agency, prompting community members to attend public meetings, submit public records requests, or advocate for policy changes. These stories demonstrate the power of audits to inspire collective action and drive positive change.

Conclusion

In conclusion, First Amendment audits are a vital tool for promoting transparency, accountability, and public trust in government institutions. By documenting interactions with public officials and sharing their findings, auditors help ensure that government actions are conducted openly and ethically. The key themes and findings from this book highlight the importance of continued efforts to promote transparency and accountability through First Amendment audits. Auditors play an essential role in safeguarding civil liberties and promoting open government, and their work has a profound impact on public awareness and engagement. Through their dedication to transparency and accountability, auditors contribute to a more open and just society, ensuring that public institutions operate with integrity and respect for citizens' rights.

The Ongoing Need for Transparency and Accountability

While First Amendment audits have made significant strides in promoting transparency and accountability, the journey is far from over. Persistent challenges and obstacles continue to confront auditors, underscoring the need for ongoing vigilance and sustained efforts. This section explores the challenges faced by auditors, the importance of continued vigilance, and future directions for First Amendment audits.

Challenges and Obstacles

Auditors often encounter a range of challenges and obstacles in their efforts to promote transparency and accountability. These challenges can stem from legal, social, and institutional resistance, making it essential for auditors to be prepared and resilient.

1. **Persistent Challenges Faced by Auditors, Including Legal and Social Obstacles**: Auditors frequently face legal challenges, such as arrests, lawsuits, and harassment, for exercising their right to record in public spaces. These legal obstacles can be daunting and require auditors to have a thorough understanding of their rights and access to legal support. Social obstacles, such as public misunderstanding and hostility, can also pose significant challenges. Auditors must navigate these social dynamics carefully to maintain public support and effectively communicate the importance of their work.
2. **Examples of Resistance from Public Officials and Institutions**: Resistance from public officials and institutions is a common challenge for auditors. For example, an auditor might be confronted by a public official who is unaware of or hostile to the legal right to record. In some cases, institutions may implement policies or practices that hinder transparency, such as restricting access to public records or limiting public participation in meetings. These examples highlight the need for auditors to be persistent and resourceful in overcoming resistance.

The Importance of Continued Vigilance

The need for transparency and accountability is ongoing, and auditors must remain vigilant to ensure that public institutions continue to operate openly and ethically. Continued audits are essential for maintaining momentum and addressing new challenges as they arise.

1. **The Need for Ongoing Audits to Ensure That Public Institutions Remain Transparent and Accountable**: Public institutions are constantly evolving, and new challenges to transparency and accountability can emerge at any time. Ongoing audits help ensure that these institutions remain subject to public scrutiny and that any issues are promptly addressed. Regular audits also reinforce the importance of transparency and accountability, reminding public officials and institutions of their obligations to the public.
2. **Strategies for Maintaining Momentum and Addressing New Challenges as They Arise**: To maintain momentum, auditors should stay informed about current events and emerging issues that may impact transparency and accountability. Building strong support networks, engaging with the community, and collaborating with other auditors can help sustain efforts and address new challenges. Additionally, auditors should continuously refine their strategies and adapt to changing circumstances to remain effective.

Future Directions for First Amendment Audits

As society and technology continue to evolve, so too must the practice of First Amendment audits. Emerging trends and areas of focus will shape the future of audits, and auditors must be prepared to adapt and innovate.

1. **Emerging Trends and Areas of Focus for Future Audits**: Future audits may focus on new areas of public concern, such as digital privacy, surveillance, and the use of technology in government operations. Auditors may also explore issues related to environmental transparency, public health, and social justice. By staying attuned to these emerging trends, auditors can ensure that their work remains relevant and impactful.
2. **The Evolving Role of Technology in Enhancing Audit Effectiveness**: Technology plays a crucial role in enhancing the effectiveness of audits. Advances in recording equipment, data analysis, and digital communication can help auditors document interactions more accurately, analyze findings more comprehensively, and share their work more widely. Embracing new technologies and staying informed about technological developments will be essential for auditors to remain effective in their efforts.

Conclusion

The ongoing need for transparency and accountability underscores the importance of First Amendment audits. Despite the challenges and obstacles faced by auditors, their work remains crucial for ensuring that public institutions operate openly and ethically. Continued vigilance and sustained efforts are essential for maintaining momentum and addressing new challenges as they arise. By staying informed, building strong support networks, and embracing new technologies, auditors can adapt to changing circumstances and continue to promote transparency and accountability. The future of First Amendment audits holds great potential for driving positive change and fostering a more open and just society. Through their dedication and perseverance, auditors contribute to a culture of transparency and accountability that benefits everyone.

Encouraging Responsible and Ethical Auditing Practices

As First Amendment auditors continue their vital work, it is crucial to emphasize the importance of conducting audits responsibly and ethically. Ethical auditing practices not only ensure the integrity of the audits but also help maintain public trust and support. This section explores best practices for auditors, strategies for building public trust, and lessons learned from successful auditors.

Best Practices for Auditors

Adhering to best practices is essential for conducting audits ethically and effectively. These guidelines help auditors navigate the complexities of their work while maintaining respect for privacy and minimizing disruptions.

1. **Guidelines for Conducting Audits Ethically and Responsibly**: Auditors should follow a set of ethical guidelines that prioritize respect for privacy and responsible recording practices. This includes avoiding the recording of private conversations, sensitive information, or areas where individuals have a reasonable expectation of privacy. Auditors should also ensure that their activities do not interfere with the normal operations of public buildings or disrupt the work of public officials.

2. **Tips for Balancing Transparency with Respect for Privacy and Minimizing Disruptions**: Balancing the need for transparency with respect for privacy is a key ethical consideration for auditors. To achieve this balance, auditors should focus on public areas and interactions that are visible from public spaces. They should avoid recording through windows or into private spaces where individuals have a reasonable expectation of privacy. Additionally, auditors should communi-

cate clearly with public officials and employees, explaining the purpose of the audit and addressing any concerns respectfully.

Building Public Trust

Maintaining public trust is essential for the success of First Amendment audits. Ethical auditing practices and positive engagement with the community help build and sustain this trust.

1. **The Importance of Maintaining Public Support Through Ethical Auditing Practices**: Public support is crucial for the effectiveness of audits. When the public trusts that auditors are acting ethically and responsibly, they are more likely to support and engage with the auditing process. Ethical auditing practices, such as respecting privacy and avoiding confrontational behavior, help build and maintain this trust.
2. **Strategies for Engaging with the Community and Fostering Positive Relationships**: Engaging with the community is essential for building positive relationships and fostering support for audits. Auditors should be transparent about their intentions, communicate clearly with the public, and address any concerns or questions respectfully. Participating in community events, hosting informational sessions, and engaging with community members on social media can also help build a network of supporters and allies.

Learning from Success Stories

Examining case studies of auditors who have successfully navigated challenges and made a positive impact can provide valuable insights and lessons. These examples highlight the importance of ethical practices and effective strategies for conducting audits.

1. **Case Studies of Auditors Who Have Successfully Navigated Challenges and Made a Positive Impact**: There are numerous examples of auditors who have conducted their work ethically and effectively, leading to positive outcomes. For instance, an auditor who conducted an audit at a public library documented interactions with staff and patrons while respecting privacy boundaries. The auditor's respectful and professional demeanor helped build trust and support for the audit, resulting in positive feedback from the community.
2. **Lessons Learned and Best Practices That Can Be Applied to Future Audits**: Successful auditors often share common practices and strategies that contribute to their effectiveness. These include thorough preparation and research, clear communication with public officials and the community, and a commitment to ethical standards. By learning from these success stories, auditors can refine their own practices and enhance the impact of their work.

Conclusion

Encouraging responsible and ethical auditing practices is essential for the success and integrity of First Amendment audits. By adhering to best practices, balancing transparency with respect for privacy, and building public trust, auditors can conduct their work ethically and effectively. Learning from the experiences of successful auditors provides valuable insights and lessons that can be applied to future audits. Through their dedication to ethical standards and responsible practices, auditors contribute to a more open and just society, ensuring that public institutions operate transparently and ethically. By fostering positive relationships with the community and maintaining public support, auditors help build a foundation for lasting change and a culture of accountability.

The Broader Impact of First Amendment Audits

First Amendment audits extend their influence far beyond individual interactions with public officials. They play a crucial role in shaping public policy, empowering citizens, and fostering a culture of accountability. This section explores the broader impact of First Amendment audits, highlighting their influence on policy and legislative reforms, their role in empowering citizens and communities, and their contribution to creating a culture of accountability.

Influence on Policy and Legislative Reforms

First Amendment audits have a significant impact on public policy and legislative reforms. By documenting and exposing issues within public institutions, auditors provide the evidence needed to drive meaningful changes in laws and policies.

1. **How Audit Findings Have Informed Policy Changes and Legislative Reforms**: Audit findings often reveal gaps in existing policies and highlight areas where reforms are needed. For example, an audit might uncover a lack of transparency in how a city council conducts its meetings. These findings can prompt policymakers to adopt new policies that ensure meetings are open to the public and that records are readily accessible. Similarly, audits that expose misconduct or inefficiencies can lead to legislative reforms aimed at improving accountability and oversight.

2. **Examples of Specific Laws and Policies That Have Been Influenced by Audit Activities**: There are numerous examples of audits leading to significant policy and legislative changes. For instance, an audit of a police department might reveal issues with how complaints against officers are handled. The documented evidence can lead to the implementation of new procedures for investigating complaints and ensuring ac-

countability. In some cases, audit findings have inspired new laws that explicitly protect the right to record in public spaces, ensuring that auditors can conduct their work without fear of legal repercussions.

Empowering Citizens and Communities

First Amendment audits play a vital role in empowering citizens and communities. By raising awareness about constitutional rights and encouraging civic participation, audits help create a more informed and active citizenry.

1. **The Role of Audits in Educating the Public and Fostering Civic Engagement**: Auditors often engage with the public during their audits, explaining the legal basis for their activities and the importance of transparency and accountability. By documenting and sharing their findings, auditors help educate the public about their rights and the role of audits in promoting open government. This increased awareness empowers individuals to exercise their rights and advocate for themselves and their communities.
2. **Stories of Communities That Have Mobilized for Change as a Result of Audit Findings**: There are numerous stories of communities that have been empowered by audit activities. For example, an audit might reveal issues with transparency in a local government agency, prompting community members to attend public meetings, submit public records requests, or advocate for policy changes. These stories demonstrate the power of audits to inspire collective action and drive positive change.

Creating a Culture of Accountability

First Amendment audits contribute to creating a broader culture of accountability within public institutions. By documenting interactions and exposing issues, auditors help ensure that public officials are held accountable for their actions.

1. **How Audits Have Contributed to a Broader Culture of Accountability Within Public Institutions**: Audits act as a deterrent to unethical behavior and encourage public officials to adhere to ethical standards. Knowing that their actions are being documented and scrutinized, officials are more likely to operate transparently and responsibly. This shift towards accountability can lead to significant improvements in government practices and policies.
2. **The Ripple Effect of Individual Audits Inspiring Broader Movements for Transparency**: Individual audits can have a far-reaching impact, inspiring others to take up the cause of transparency and accountability. The actions of one auditor can set off a chain reaction, leading to broader movements and systemic changes. For example, an auditor who exposes corruption in a local government might inspire community members to conduct their own audits and advocate for reforms. Similarly, an auditor who documents police misconduct might motivate others to monitor law enforcement practices and push for greater accountability.

Conclusion

The broader impact of First Amendment audits is evident in their influence on policy and legislative reforms, their role in empowering citizens and communities, and their contribution to creating a culture of accountability. By documenting and exposing issues within public institutions, auditors provide the evidence needed to drive meaningful changes in laws and policies. Audits also play a vital role in educating the public and fostering civic engagement, empowering individuals to exercise their rights and advocate for their communities. Through their dedication to transparency and accountability, auditors contribute to a more open and just society, ensuring that public institutions operate with integrity and respect for citizens' rights. The ripple effect of individual audits inspires broader movements for transparency and accountability, creating a lasting impact that benefits everyone.

Final Thoughts and Call to Action

As we conclude this exploration of First Amendment audits, it is essential to reflect on the ongoing importance of these activities and the role they play in promoting transparency and accountability. This final section emphasizes the need for continued efforts, ways to support auditors, and a call to action for readers to stay informed, get involved, and support open government initiatives.

The Importance of Continued Efforts

The work of First Amendment auditors is far from complete. As society evolves and new challenges emerge, the need for transparency and accountability remains as critical as ever. Auditors must continue their efforts to ensure that public institutions operate openly and ethically.

1. **The Ongoing Need for Auditors to Promote Transparency and Accountability**: Public institutions are constantly changing, and new issues related to transparency and accountability can arise at any time. Continued audits help ensure that these institutions remain subject to public scrutiny and that any problems are promptly addressed. Regular audits reinforce the importance of transparency and ac-

countability, reminding public officials of their obligations to the public.
2. **Encouragement for New Auditors to Join the Movement and Contribute to Positive Change**: The movement for transparency and accountability needs new voices and perspectives. Aspiring auditors are encouraged to join the effort, bringing their unique skills and insights to the cause. By becoming involved, new auditors can contribute to positive change and help build a more open and just society.

Supporting Auditors and Their Work

Supporting the work of First Amendment auditors is crucial for ensuring their continued success and impact. There are several ways that the public, organizations, and policymakers can support auditors and their efforts.

1. **Ways the Public Can Support Auditors, Including Advocacy, Legal Support, and Community Engagement**: Members of the public can support auditors by advocating for their rights, providing legal assistance, and engaging with their work. This can include attending public meetings, sharing audit findings on social media, and offering financial or legal support to auditors facing challenges. Community engagement is also vital, as it helps build a network of supporters and allies who can amplify the impact of audits.
2. **The Role of Organizations and Policymakers in Supporting Audit Activities**: Organizations and policymakers play a critical role in supporting audit activities. Civil liberties organizations can provide resources, training, and legal assistance to auditors. Policymakers can enact laws and policies that protect the right to record in public spaces and ensure

that public institutions operate transparently. By working together, organizations and policymakers can create an environment that supports and encourages the work of auditors.

Looking Ahead

The future of First Amendment audits holds great potential for continued impact. As technology evolves and new challenges emerge, auditors must adapt and innovate to remain effective. This section looks ahead to the future of audits and provides a call to action for readers.

1. **The Future of First Amendment Audits and the Potential for Continued Impact**: Advances in technology, such as improved recording equipment and digital communication tools, offer new opportunities for auditors to document interactions and share their findings. Future audits may also focus on emerging issues, such as digital privacy, surveillance, and environmental transparency. By staying attuned to these trends, auditors can ensure that their work remains relevant and impactful.
2. **A Call to Action for Readers to Stay Informed, Get Involved, and Support Efforts to Promote Open Government**: Readers are encouraged to stay informed about issues related to transparency and accountability, get involved in their communities, and support efforts to promote open government. This can include attending public meetings, advocating for policy changes, and supporting the work of auditors. By taking action, readers can contribute to a culture of transparency and accountability that benefits everyone.

Conclusion

In conclusion, First Amendment audits are a vital tool for promoting transparency, accountability, and public trust in government institutions. The ongoing efforts of auditors are essential for ensuring that public institutions operate openly and ethically. By supporting auditors, staying informed, and getting involved, readers can contribute to a more open and just society. The future of First Amendment audits holds great potential for continued impact, and it is up to all of us to support and sustain these efforts. Together, we can build a culture of transparency and accountability that benefits everyone and ensures that government actions are conducted in the public interest.

Milton Keynes UK
Ingram Content Group UK Ltd.
UKHW031634201124
451457UK00011B/223